The Long Walk with Little Amal

Thousands and thousands of children were among the crowds all along the roads that Little Amal took on her 8000-kilometre journey from the Syrian border with Turkey to the heart of England. Their memories will not fade; the joy and excitement, the wide-eyed delight will last, always, with everyone of all ages whose path she crossed on beaches, in city squares, on country roads. Perhaps too for the many millions more who read of her events and concerts or saw them in the media.

Amal, the magnificent puppet, and all of those who brought her on this unmatchable expedition will be forever the object of affection and admiration.

Distinguished writers from every country through which the miraculous Amal passed have joined eminent photographers to create their record and this tribute to an unmatchable expedition. Their testimonies are sometimes angry and often a painful account of the unending suffering of refugees searching for a new life in Europe. They also are a beautiful and moving, even playful, homage to the courage of those who have risked their lives to make this journey and an overwhelming call to make this puppet and every child she stands for welcome.

The Long Walk with Little Amal

*The Walk Productions
and
Good Chance Theatre
and
Handspring Puppet Company*

MOUNTAIN LEOPARD PRESS
WELBECK · LONDON

First published in 2021 by

Mountain Leopard Press
an imprint of Welbeck Publishing Group
20 Mortimer Street,
London W1T 3JW

www.mountainleopard.press

9 8 7 6 5 4 3 2 1

THE LONG WALK WITH LITTLE AMAL in collaboration with The Walk Productions, Good Chance Theatre and Handspring Puppet Company, with an introduction by Amir Nizar Zuabi and an afterword by David Lan. Photography by André Liohn, Abdul Saboor, Nicolas Dupraz, Simon Annand, David Levene and Zozan Yaşar.

Introduction © Amir Nizar Zuabi, 2021

Afterword © David Lan, 2021

Original texts © Samar Yazbek, 2021; ©Burhan Sönmez, 2021;
© Laura Jansen, 2021; © Erri De Luca, 2021;
© Philippe Claudel, 2021; © Tuesday Reitano, 2021;
© Timur Vermes, 2021; © Marieke Lucas Rijneveld, 2021;
© Olivier Norek, 2021; © Cressida Cowell, 2021

Translation of texts: © Jonathan Wright of Samar Yazbek, 2021;
© N. S. Thompson of Erri De Luca, 2021;
© Stephanie Smee of Philippe Claudel, 2021;
© Jamie Bulloch of Timur Vermes, 2021;
© Michele Hutchison of Marieke Lucas Rijneveld, 2021;
© Nick Caistor of Olivier Norek, 2021

Maps © Emily Faccini, 2021

Design & layout © Mountain Leopard Press

Photographs:
© André Liohn, 2021, Syria–Turkey Border: all images;
Turkey: all images; Greece: all images; Italy: pp. 64–7

© Abdul Saboor, 2021, Italy: p. 58, pp. 60–3, p. 68, pp. 70–3;
France – South: p. 74, pp. 78–84, pp. 86–7; Germany:
all images; Belgium / The Netherlands: all images;
France – North: all images

© Nicolas Dupraz, 2021, Switzerland: all images

© Simon Annand, 2021, U.K.: p. 138, p. 140

© Dan Kitwood/Getty Images, 2021, U.K.: p. 141

© David Levene, 2021, U.K.: pp. 142–6, p. 147 (above), pp. 148–9

© Zozan Yaşar, 2021, U.K.: pp. 151–5

© Sarah Loader, 2021, Italy: p. 69

© Mountain Leopard Press, 2021, France – South: p. 85;
U.K.: p. 147 (below), p. 150

The moral right of Samar Yazbek, Burhan Sönmez, Laura Jansen, Erri De Luca, Philippe Claudel, Tuesday Reitano, Timur Vermes, Marieke Lucas Rijneveld, Olivier Norek, Cressida Cowell, Amir Nizar Zuabi and David Lan to be recognised as the authors of this work has been asserted in accordance with the Copyright, Designs and Patents Act, 1988.

A CIP catalogue record for this book is available from the British Library

ISBN 978-1-91449-528-1

Designed and typeset in Scala by Libanus Press Ltd, Marlborough
Printed and bound in Great Britain by Bell & Bain Ltd, Glasgow

FSC
www.fsc.org

MIX
Paper from
responsible sources
FSC® C007785

Introduction

AMIR NIZAR ZUABI

When David Lan first told me about his idea to walk from Syria to the U.K. accompanying a 3.5-metre giant girl named Amal I was immediately in love.

At that early stage it was a very unstructured idea and I didn't know that this conversation in a small café in Soho, London would very shortly devour my life.

I am a theatre maker from Palestine. I have worked for many years creating shows that thread carefully between the poetic and the political. My decision was to create art that talks about today, about the circumstances I was in but within a prism of poetry in order that the shows would not fall victim to the trap of reductivity which is often the case with political theatre.

I wanted my shows to be about people not slogans. I wanted my writing to be about possibilities not alliances.

So when David told me about Amal I imagined a pilgrimage.

I imagined the theatrical potential of a gentle giant roaming the streets.

I immediately imagined the power of giving a huge shadow to what is usually portrayed as small and vulnerable.

Now The Walk has happened and it has been much more than anything I could have imagined.

This was a voyage through many communities, through many cultures, through many rhythms, but at the same time it was all about one thing: it was about generosity, it was about the act of giving something of yourself not in order to receive something back, but in order to become part of something big and that big thing that united all these communities, diverse as they were, was a deep sense of compassion.

Compassion has become an unfashionable word, but now more than ever in a world becoming more and more polarised it is needed.

We walked with a puppet – a puppet with a story – but what gave this odyssey meaning was the hundreds of thousands of people we met along the way. It was they who gave this puppet, this sophisticated piece of furniture, life.

When one looks at a puppet one has to make a huge effort to let go of reality.

One needs to decipher the thoughts of an inanimate object and the only way that can happen is if one is willing to empathise and to project one's own thoughts into the puppet.

In this way Amal was nothing but a means by which our audience could rethink and renegotiate their attitudes towards others.

To our great joy we met many people who were willing to do this.

On a street corner in Marseille an elderly woman cried out to Amal as we were passing: "Be safe, my sweet daughter".

Folded into her voice was pain beyond recognition and longing that could stop a river. I looked back. I saw an old woman with big brown eyes in a head scarf. I asked her who she was.

She smiled and said, "I am a mother, a Syrian mother".

She needed to say nothing more. We were both fighting back tears. We stood silently for a long time counting our lost loved ones. As I started to walk away she whispered, "Make sure my girl is safe. Promise".

I wanted to tell her Amal isn't real.

I couldn't, maybe because by then I wasn't sure Amal isn't real.

By then Amal was the personification of hope for too many people not to be real.

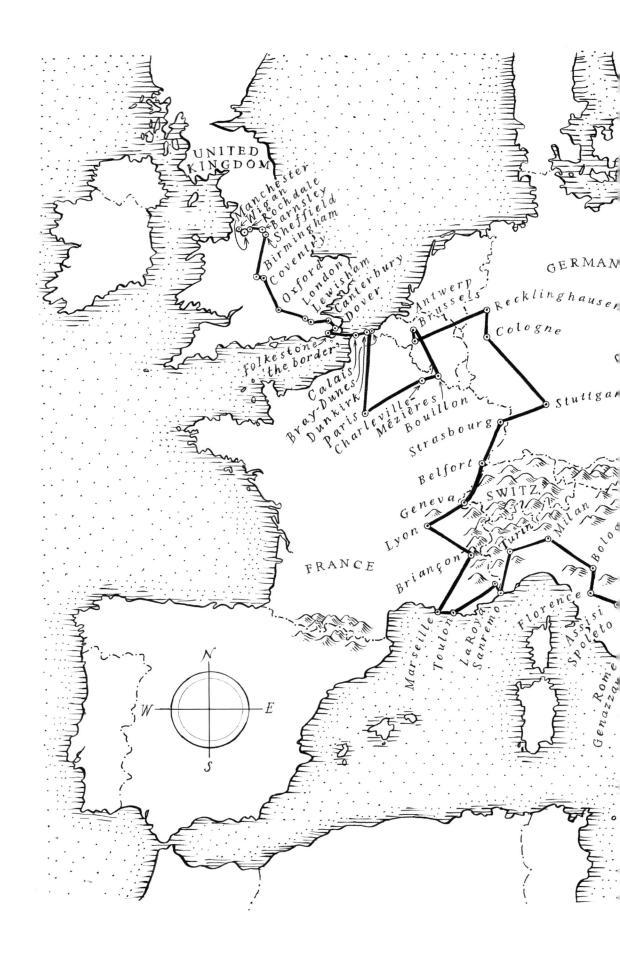

UNITED
KINGDOM

Manchester
Wigan
Rochdale
Barnsley
Sheffield
Birmingham
Coventry

Oxford
London
Lewisham
Canterbury
Dover

Folkestone
'the border'
Calais
Bray-Dunes
Dunkirk
Paris
Charleville-
Mézières
Bouillon

Antwerp
Brussels

Recklinghausen
Cologne

GERMAN

Stuttgar

Strasbourg

Belfort

Geneva
Lyon
SWITZ.

Briançon
Turin
Milan

FRANCE

Marseille
Toulon
La Roya
Sanremo
Florence
Assisi
Spoleto
Genazza
Rome
Bolo

N
W — E
S

The Long Walk with Little Amal

Syria–Turkey Border

SAMAR YAZBEK

Justice for Little Amal

The low hills on the Turkish-Syrian border have been a lifeline for Syrians seeking safe haven from the horrors of a decade of war. One day in August 2013, I was there in a large crowd of people waiting – young and old, some families complete, others reduced by war. The sun was scorching hot. I waited with the women at the checkpoint manned by the Islamist forces. I had to get through before we could go up into those hills. At my side was a young mother carrying her baby and by her side a girl of six clutching her mother's dress. The girl and I exchanged fleeting glances. She wasn't the same age as Little Amal who is now travelling through Europe. She was a little younger. I tried to draw her into conversation, but she looked frightened and temperamental. I guessed that she too was waiting to walk through the hills though I couldn't be sure because she and her mother disappeared within an hour and I didn't see her when we crossed the border clandestinely. In the queue she was standing by my side, with dust all over her black trousers and in her short and boyish flaxen hair. Her mother told me that their house had been bombed and her husband killed and she was now travelling with her brother. The mother was no more than 25 years old – a slim, beautiful woman in a headscarf that she lifted up from time to time. We stood in line like soldiers, and we could still hear explosions in the distance. I decided to speak to the little girl, who was avoiding me and taking cover in her mother's skirts. I started playing a game with her – I would hide my head behind her mother's back, then pop out on the other side laughing. But the little girl didn't smile. Her face showed no reaction. She tried to escape my teasing, which annoyed her. I didn't give up, although the sun was at its zenith and our faces were dripping with sweat. The saltiness was irritating on our skin and I saw how the girl was writhing in discomfort. I felt that we were all in the same boat – the war had taken a frightening turn, I.S.I.S. columns were moving into Syria and Islamist forces controlled the areas that had previously been liberated by the Free Syrian Army. International intervention had hijacked what began as an uprising by the Syrian people, leading to open warfare. I hadn't yet written my book *The Crossing*, but I was carrying much of the material I had collected in my suitcase, including

Opposite: The border

The border

interviews with children the same age as this girl, children I had lived with in shelters or visited in hospitals or sometimes whose bodies I had carried after they were killed. I tried to speak to the mother again. She replied with a sigh and said that her brother had gone on ahead with their papers. I asked her about her daughter and she said she had hardly spoken for a year. She said this as if it were almost normal, part of a normality I was used to and of which I had become a part. The little girl stopped speaking most of the time when she was five years old, when their house was bombed and she escaped with her mother and father. For a while she might say a few words, her mother told me, then added: "After her father was killed by a shell in the market, she lost the ability to speak altogether." The girl could hear us and was looking at me inquisitively. My sunglasses hid

my eyes and I was worried I might cry. Actually crying would seem stupid amid such tragedies. The day before I had seen a beautiful five-year-old boy lying in hospital with a black mark the size of a pea on his lower stomach where a piece of shrapnel from a cluster bomb had hit him. The boy died and I didn't cry. I just heard a clicking sound in my throat. So there I was, looking at the girl who wouldn't speak and thinking of the boy who had died yesterday without so much as a groan. In the distance a man waved and shouted and the mother ran off, with the girl running after her, and then they disappeared into the crowd. That girl might have been called Amal.

An hour later, as we climbing the hill through the woods I found another girl about eight years old by my side. She was scrambling up the hill with us to get into Turkish territory. We could hear gunfire: the

A young Afghan refugee searching through rubbish in Van, eastern Turkey

Afghan refugees in Van, eastern Turkey

Turkish gendarmes were firing at refugees trying to cross the border and we could hear screams in the woods. The girl was single-mindedly moving forward on her elbows. Her eyes didn't look like a child's eyes. They were hard eyes, full of a savage fear. In them I could see death. Her long hair was hanging loose around her, picking up the dust, and she was sweating. I tried to get close to her, but she moved away. Her mother was right behind her, looking at me anxiously. The guide ahead of us was gesturing at us, asking us to make no noise. The girl was the best of us at scrambling between the low thorny bushes. Then I saw that one of her shoes had slipped off, but I couldn't pick it up. She just left it and moved on. She had no socks and I noticed that her toes were bleeding. When we reached the top of the hill and slipped down the other side towards the Turkish border, I caught sight of the girl at a distance, sliding down the slope in a seated position. Then she disappeared and I never saw her again because I had to keep my head down for fear of bullets. I didn't know that girl's name either, but I could readily call her Amal, like the girl travelling through Europe and crossing borders as a symbol of all the children who have had to flee Syria and take refuge in neighbouring countries – in Turkey, Lebanon, Jordan or European countries, children who have travelled by sea or in planes, who have crossed land borders or who have lost their homes and taken refuge elsewhere inside Syria, and those who have drowned at sea.

As she crosses European borders, visits cities and meets politicians and children, does anyone ask Little Amal why she is there? Why her face bears such marks of sorrow and pain. Or why she has to be so gigantic. Is she like that so that others will look at her and notice her pain, and then say: "Yes, she's a Syrian refugee." She brings you a story of a tragedy taking place in the world. Can you look away and ignore the pains of others?

I met Little Amal at the Institut du Monde Arabe in Paris and held her hand. She was surrounded by children who gave her messages, and showed solidarity. She then played hide-and-seek with them, and the French media said that the purpose of the Little Amal project was to publicise the tragedy of Syrian child refugees, but wait a moment: why is Amal here? Why is she crossing borders and making such a vast journey? Do I have to go through the same thing again and again – with another Syrian girl crossing borders? Why do we, and Little Amal too, have to turn the Syrian tragedy into a piece of theatre that is permanently on tour, simply to make the world understand the horrors we have seen? Will the world one day look into the eyes of the children who are victims and say: "We apologise." I don't think so. But I do think it's important to talk and that while Little Amal is making her journeys we also tell them why Amal and thousands of other Syrian children are in exile, why there are more than two and a half million Syrian children who have had no education, and why a child such as Hamza al-Khatib was killed in 2011. Hamza was born in 1997 in the town of Daraa, arrested and tortured to death by the Bashar al-Assad regime on April 29, 2011. He was thirteen. When his family received his body, they found his penis had been cut off, that his neck had been broken and he had been shot in several places. There are also the children that I.S.I.S. recruited when it held parts of Syria. I.S.I.S. gave them a choice between fighting and dying. Can we say why this happened to children?

Little Amal is a refugee in Europe for political reasons and not because of a natural disaster. Little Amal travels around with her sad face because a popular movement arose in her country to demand legal and constitutional reforms, such as the repeal of emergency law and the release of political prisoners. Young Amal is fed up with being seen as something strange! She wants to explain to the world that in Syria she was deprived of the most basic rights of

Afghan refugees in Van, eastern Turkey

children – shelter, housing, food and drink. I won't even mention education because someone who has nothing to eat or drink and who doesn't have a house does not have the luxury of talking about education.

In my book *A Woman in the Crossfire* I wrote about two children who were alone in a demonstration in Marjeh Square in Damascus in March 2011. The authorities had detained their father, who had been demonstrating to demand the release of their mother. Later I wrote about children in the countryside around Idlib in northern Syria. Then I decided not to talk about children. I felt I was taking advantage of their suffering and it was too painful. I decided to leave children out of my project documenting the uprising and the war. It would be a feminist project narrated by women, I told myself.

I preferred to speak to adults because they under-stood that they were giving testimony. After that it was difficult to go back and talk about Little Amal and other girls like her. My greatest fear is that our portrayal of the victims' pain might be voyeuristic. I don't want that to happen to Little Amal now. I don't want her to be a transitory, ephemeral moment – a moment that trivialises the humanitarian urge. This happens when we sympathise with children but forget the source of their suffering. Maybe many people will respond to Amal by donating to the camps or writing posts on social media. The news agencies and big newspapers might cover the Little Amal story, but what Amal may want, and here I am saying what I believe as a Syrian like her, is that the world should know why she was forced to leave her country. So maybe I should now tell you in a few words a small chapter of her story:

Little Amal wasn't born when the popular unrest began in Syria. When she was born the war had already begun. Amal didn't know what was happening around her. She didn't know that the regime had suppressed peaceful demonstrations or that foreign powers had started to intervene. She doesn't know anything about the children gassed in Ghouta in 2013. When she came into this world she saw it with eyes full of joy, but fear and suffering soon left their marks on her face. She may have stayed in camps, she may have crossed the border with her mother like that girl who lost her shoe in the woods, she may have come to Europe by sea, hopefully without ending up dead on the beach like young Alan Kurdi. She may have seen her house bombed or shelled, or she may have left home with her family because of poverty and hunger in the areas controlled by the Assad government. Amal may have lived through many misfortunes without telling the world about them, but she travels the world and asks it to look into her eyes, thinking that the world will understand her sadness and will see what has befallen her people. Little Amal does not know that images of victims do not tell us much, or that ignoring the tragedy the world has inflicted on her and on other children has gone hand in hand with the process of plundering her country's resources and dividing them up between various states. Little Amal does not know whether justice will be served one day or whether those who have committed war crimes will ever be held to account. She would like to enjoy a little peace and save what can be saved of the lives of the many children who are like her. She does not want to make speeches. She does not want to explain herself in books or research papers or send political messages to the United Nations. She no longer believes and doesn't want to take part in all this pain. She just walks and her face tells the story, a story that humanity has known since humanity began, the story of war, the story of children who are waiting for us to see their future as part of a new humane future, a future that is mysterious and fraught with dangers. Will anyone look into Amal's face and strive for justice for her and other children?

Translated from the Arabic by Jonathan Wright

Above, opposite and overleaf: Little Amal in Gaziantep, Turkey, which has a high-population of Syrian refugees. Little Amal was greeted by crowds lighting her way with lanterns

The cemetery for unidentified Afghan refugees in Van, eastern Turkey

A candyfloss seller in Adana, Turkey

Amal is surrounded by birds on the bridge over the river Seyhan in Adana

A group of Afghan refugees hiding under a bridge in the city of Tatvan, eastern Turkey

Above and overleaf: Amal in the historic city of Tarsus

Turkey

BURHAN SÖNMEZ

Six Years Ago

Little Amal as an idea was born six years ago, when Joe Robertson joined Joe Murphy and Tracey Seaward to go to the refugee camp in Calais together. Thousands of refugees were massed in a tent city, looking for opportunities to cross from France to the U.K. That created an idea and four theatre directors founded Good Chance and tried to share the hope of thousands of people through the medium of a little girl. Amal is one of the ten thousand people in the tent city of refugees. The tent city amounts to a tiny proportion of the eighty two million refugees around the world. Eighty-two million is more than the population of most countries. But they have neither country nor a home. Many do not even have tents.

Amal turns the road into a stage. Shakespeare's phrase "All the world's a stage" is given a new meaning. Where the world is big, the stage can be big, Amal shows this and says "Don't forget about us". The only way not to be forgotten is to leave a trace. To leave a mark on the road with giant steps, to leave a mark in the minds and hearts of people.

Two Months Ago

Kurdish families who came to work in the city of Afyon in southern Turkey were attacked. Seven people were injured. Whole families were forced to leave the city under military protection. In the capital, Ankara, a Kurdish family was targeted and four people were injured. In Konya, in the centre of Turkey, a Kurdish family was assaulted and one person was killed. Hatred of the "other" in Turkey did not begin with the arrival of Syrian or Afghan immigrants. The oppression, exclusion and violence against Kurdish families who have gone to work from eastern cities to other parts of Turkey, especially in the summer, to work in agriculture, are a continuation of it. Kurds make up a quarter of the population of Turkey and their national rights – such as the right to be educated in Kurdish – are ignored. The demands of the Kurds lead to their marginalisation as a nation. This makes seasonal Kurdish workers cheaper to employ.

Two months ago, photographs of illegal immigrants entering Turkey from the Iranian border were published, and a xenophobia campaign became popular both in the press and on social media. Foreigners on the street became a target. Musab Yousef, a Palestinian journalist who has lived in Turkey for

Opposite: Amal in Mersin

Opposite and above: Afghan refugees in an abandoned house in Van, Turkey in August 2021, hiding from Turkish police. They had fled Afghanistan and the Taliban five weeks earlier

many years, was beaten, after eating at a restaurant, for protesting when he saw that extra food was added to the bill. He was beaten and injured while told, "Go home, go back to your country, dirty immigrant." The "xenophobia" spreading into daily life and the practice of profiting from foreigners go hand in hand. Immigrants from Asia and Africa are used as cheap workers in every sector, from textile to farming, to increase the profits of businesses in Turkey. Migrant workers mean cheap labour, cheaper than the Kurds.

July 20, 2021
World Refugee Day. It has been celebrated around the world since 2001. The United Nations took this decision on the fiftieth anniversary of the 1951 Convention Relating to the Status of Refugees.

On World Refugee Day, a Pakistani immigrant named Huseyin, who has been living in Turkey for seven years, told a journalist: "I can't go to the hospital. Because I have no records, no documents. Thankfully, I have not been so ill so far. I pray that I don't get ill."

A refugee should not get ill, be very hungry, read too much, talk too much, not look too much. If she is like a puppet, she will be safe, as Little Amal is safe.

Six Years Ago
Alan Kurdi, a three-year-old Syrian Kurdish boy, drowned in the Mediterranean Sea with his mother and brother and his dead body appeared in all the news. His family came to Turkey fleeing the war in Syria. They couldn't return to their home. Instead,

when the attacks of I.S.I.S. increased, they tried to cross the Mediterranean and go to Europe. Their ultimate goal was to go to their relatives in Canada. The Kurdi family gave $5,860 to the smugglers and got on the boat, sailing from southern Turkey at dusk. Sixteen people were on the eight man boat, and their life jackets were not functioning.

Alan Kurdi's body was found, he was lucky, the bodies of many immigrants were lost in the Mediterranean. Eight hundred migrants died trying to cross the Mediterranean in the first half of 2021 alone. The exact number cannot be known. There are those who estimate their number to be ten thousand or thirty thousand or fifty thousand. Now Little Amal is trying to cross the waters that they could not cross. She travels without counting numbers, only collecting the hopes of the dead.

Angela Merkel

The Chancellor of Germany made statements at her traditional summer press conference. "Turkey takes very good care of Syrian refugees," she said. After praising Turkey for keeping refugees within its borders, she said, "I don't think Turkey can become a member of the E.U."

Merkel stated that she was in favour of the continuation of the migration agreement between the E.U. and Turkey, and recalled that at the last E.U. leaders' Summit this year, it was decided to give three billion euros to Turkey for taking care of immigrants. She stated that she had talks with Turkish President Recep Tayyip Erdoğan on these issues. Pointing out that immigrants should not be used as a political tool, Merkel said, "Turkey takes very good care of Syrian refugees, in particular. It does an incredible number of things there. We have supported Turkey. I want this agreement to be developed. This is the best for the people affected." Referring to the E.U.'s asylum policy, Merkel pointed out that the E.U. still has not developed a common asylum policy and noted that

this is a great burden for the E.U. and needs to be resolved.

In 2015, the E.U. provided three billion euros of funding for Syrians in Turkey, and then in 2021, it was decided to create an additional three billion-euro fund. Thanks to a total of six billion euros in refugee aid, an agreement was reached with Erdoğan, who established a dictatorship in Turkey, and both sides benefited from it.

Opposition parties have accused Erdoğan's government of selling Turkey to Europe by making it the subject of a refugee bargain. The xenophobia that already existed among the people has been increasing.

Twenty Years Ago

The U.S.A. bombed Afghanistan. More than forty countries, including all N.A.T.O. countries, supported the United States. By the end of two decades, the Taliban had taken control of the country as the occupying forces withdrew. A new wave of immigration has begun. It is estimated that there are four hundred thousand Afghan immigrants in Turkey alone.

While the U.S.A. and its allies were preparing to leave Afghanistan, a dialogue with Turkey was developed at the N.A.T.O. summit in 2021. It was decided that Turkish soldiers would take on the task of guarding the airport in Kabul. It is not known what was given to Turkey in return for this agreement. An agreement that was cancelled by the arrival of the Taliban.

Ten Years Ago

The civil war in Syria has turned into a war mostly involving foreign powers. While the instigator of this war was I.S.I.S. and similar organisations, its antagonists were western countries, especially the U.S.A., and countries in the Middle East, among them Turkey and Saudi Arabia. Half of Syria's population became migrants. They fled to countries including

Little Amal resting in the small village of Musali, watched over by the villagers who received her

Turkey, Lebanon, Jordan, Egypt and Iraq. Thirteen million Syrians have been displaced since the beginning of the conflict, including those displaced internally. In Turkey alone, their number reached five million. Now in Turkey the concept of "guest immigrant" was coined in official and everyday language. People call millions of foreigners "guest", and now want them to leave.

The Austrian Chancellor

Austrian former Chancellor Sebastian Kurz warned the European Union about the new wave of immigration from Afghanistan with the withdrawal of U.S. troops.

Kurz, in an interview to *Bild*, said, "neighbouring countries or Turkey are the right places for Afghan refugees. If people have to flee, I definitely see countries like Turkey as the right place, rather than everybody coming to Austria, Germany or Sweden." He said that he's pleased because the line followed by Europe and Germany in 2015 against irregular migration has changed. He added, "As the European Union, we must be active starting from the summer season in order to prevent the recurrence of the situation of that period."

Since the Turkish government has agreed with the European Union on this issue, it keeps immigrants within its borders in exchange for some money and a lot of political tolerance. Partly for this reason, the Erdoğan government's oppressive power and unjust policies do not receive serious reactions from European politicians.

Opposite, above and overleaf: Amal watches hot air balloons in Cappadocia

Eighty-eight Years Ago

Albert Einstein was a refugee. When the news broke that he would not return to Germany, German newspapers had headlines: "Good news! Einstein is not coming back!"

Karl Marx was a refugee. The prophet Muhammad was a refugee. Immigration knows no borders in the world or in history.

The philosopher Theodor Adorno, who fled the Nazis at the same time as Einstein, was also a refugee. "For someone who no longer has a homeland, writing becomes a place to live," he said.

Twenty-one Years Ago

After staying in the U.K. for a year and receiving treatment by way of the "Freedom from Torture" foundation, I returned to Turkey. The hope of the immigrant is that everything will get better soon and they will return home. Bertolt Brecht, another immigrant who fled the Nazis, says in one of his poems: "No need to drive a nail into the wall to hang your hat on, When you come in, just drop it on the chair." The immigrant is always ready to return. I returned with hope to Istanbul from London, and I stayed there for a year with that belief. But it wasn't long before I was sentenced to imprisonment, and at the same time my health once more got worse. When I left for the second time, I believed that I would never return to my country. Because I thought that my health would not improve and I would die abroad after a while. Before I left, I spent the last week in my home town with my parents. I told them that I

Amal at sunset

was going abroad for my business as a lawyer, and that I would be back after staying for a while. I stayed up late at night with my mother for a whole week. I had brought a tape recorder with me. My mother recited all the Kurdish fairy tales she told us in the village when we were little, I had her sing all the songs. When I took refuge in Britain, I had nothing but these tapes of my mother's voice with me. I started writing novels in exile. In my second novel, *Sins & Innocents*, I told about the love of two immigrants, one from Turkey the other from Iran, who met in Cambridge. I tried to show how those immigrants cling to life. I was an ordinary immigrant. I held on to life like everyone else. I had to hold on. Because the boat called life had overturned and I was trying to stay afloat in the waves. At that time, writing novels became my life jacket.

Tokyo Olympic Games

This year, twenty-nine athletes represented the Refugee Olympic Team, which first competed in the 2016 Rio Games. The Refugee Olympic Team is composed of athletes from eleven countries who have been living and training in thirteen host countries. They compete in twelve sports.

The flag of the Refugee Olympic Team is inspired by life jackets. Light orange with a black horizontal band, its colours represent the inflatable vests that refugees use to escape to a safer life. The person who designed the flag is a Syrian refugee named Yara Said who now lives in Amsterdam. She describes the flag, "If you wore a life jacket as a refugee, it would be very meaningful for you to see this flag. This is a very powerful memory."

The International Olympic Committee does not

Amal continues her journey through Turkey

allow athletes to carry these flags on their jerseys during competition.

A Patriot

The mayor of the city of Bolu, in the central part of Turkey, exacerbated the recent wave of xenophobia. He does not want immigrants in the city, he says. "We want them to leave, but still they do not. As a result, the water bills of foreigners in the city will be ten times more expensive." This statement drew fierce reaction. Thirty N.G.O.'s published a statement in protest. The mayor challenged that too. "I know they will call me a fascist, I don't care," he said and added, "while our soldiers are martyred in Syria, Syrians are walking around in our cities."

As Samuel Johnson wrote two centuries ago in his *Dictionary*: "Patriotism is the last refuge of a scoundrel." Politicians have sprung up waving this

Above, opposite and overleaf: Amal and her puppeteers resting in the forest outside Urla

particular flag all over the world. The crowds who live under the protection of this flag express their xenophobia with sincere patriotism. That's why their tongues are sharp.

The foreigner here is not just the person coming from another country, but the "other". In America, the other might be black, might be Mexican. In England, in line with Brexit, it is European. In Europe, it is Turk, Arab, African.

Hate, wrapped in the veil of patriotism, never questions itself. The Turkish mayor does not ask what the Turkish soldiers are looking for in Syria, or Afghanistan. He does not ask why the Turkish parliament sends troops to Syria every year, with the full support of the opposition party, but he hates the ordinary Syrian who flees the war. He does not want to see that he is himself a part of the problems that pushed Syrians towards his city.

Little Amal in the Kemeralti Bazaar, Izmir. She is greeted by six new puppet friends made by local refugee children

July 27, 2021

Little Amal started her journey on the Syrian border of Turkey. Her path may be full of enmity, hatred and misunderstanding. But this is the world we live in and yet there are good people everywhere. After an event where fairy tales were told, she went on her way to other cities and countries. Her mother is somewhere out there; she is in a sound, in a scent, or in a footprint. Amal will collect them and save them in fairy tales. Then she will ask us: "Are you ready to help a refugee girl who has come to your street?"

Little Amal at the seashore in Çeşme looking towards Greece. The shoes placed around her on the beach represent all those who have passed through the city during the refugee crisis, paying tribute to those who lost their lives crossing the Mediterranean

Greece

LAURA JANSEN

Paper boats dip and slide down the hastily-dug trenches that cut through the side of the hill between the tents. The rain comes fast and hard, collecting in pools, mixing with garbage and raw sewage, forming a sudden river of waste that the children instinctively stomp and splash in. They giggle in their mismatched shoes and garbage bag ponchos while their parents scramble to salvage the tarps flapping and ripping in the wind over their shelters.

This is Moria, on the Greek island of Lesbos. Moria, the camp that never should have been, yet kept existing year after year. Bursting at the gates until the gates could not hold. Spilling over into the surrounding hills and olive groves where a second city grew between the trees. A city of tents, of wooden crate shanties, of dark and scary corners where rats and snakes crawl over the blankets. In the summer unbearably hot and fetid, in the winter so cold that some children froze to death.

Lesbos has been the epicentre of the European refugee crisis since 2015. Seventy kilometres long, forty-seven wide and only six kilometers from the Turkish coast, it has always been a gateway to Europe in one form or another. In 2015, however, the war

in Syria and the security situation in Afghanistan reached such proportions that hundreds of thousands of men, women and children found no option but to trust their fate to human smugglers so as to escape to safety. They were forced, often at gunpoint, into overcrowded rubber dinghies, pushed into the waves and pointed in the direction of Lesbos' grey and rocky shore. Many of these voyages ended in tragedy, as the boats tipped over in the waves and currents.

Opposite: Unpacking for an evening event in Ioannina, Greece

Preparing for the first event in Greece

Amal is helped to stand before she lands in Chios

The smugglers' counterfeit life vests, filled with paper, hay or the foam used for insulation, were an illusion, and many lives have been lost in the narrow straits that divide our continent from theirs.

In the northern village of Skala Sikamineas, the Greek grandmothers, the yayas, were the first to make for the beaches and help when boats began arriving. They cradled babies and handed out milk and bread to the famished families. The villages here are dependent mostly on tourism and fishing, and the weathered fishermen respect the law of the sea. When a boat is in distress there is no choice but to help. That was the natural and human response to so much suffering and the islanders of Lesbos became an example to the world of true Philoxenia, friend to a stranger.

The numbers of those coming ashore reached unmanageable proportions in 2015, the year I came to the island. The roads and towns and hastily contrived camps were overwhelmed.

In the beginning the situation was acute, already an emergency. Tens of thousands of wet and cold human beings needed basic food, shelter, information and support. All along the coastal roads volunteers and locals kept watch, trying to help each fragile dinghy as it struggled to reach the shore. The beaches were littered with life vests, emergency blankets and clothes. We built fires at points along the coast where it was safe to land, we swept our flashlights over the waves in the hopes of catching a reflection of a life vest.

Boats that arrived at night appeared without warning. We scrambled to get to them as the faint light of a mobile pierced the dark. When the sun began to rise it was possible to search with binoculars and prepare for those who would land at dawn. What starts as a small orange hump in the distance, dipping and disappearing between the waves is eventually a perilously crowded boat coming our way. We formed cordons in the water and tried to guide them towards us, shouting and waving until we had their attention.

And then you are face to face with the thing you have only read about. The sides of the inflatables are slick with vomit. The mixture of relief and terror palpable in the faces looking at you. Women and children are huddled together at the bottom of the dinghy, the men perched on the sides. We help them get safely to land. Babies are shoved into your arms as you try to keep your balance in the water. Expressionless little faces with wet hair and blue lips stare at you in wonderment as you try to look cheerful and hand them on to the next volunteer. Over the sides come the injured, the elderly, the fragile and the weak. They come seasick and exhausted, they come jubilant and elated. Every one a story, everyone someone in need of attention and care yet the numbers are always too huge to do more than a swift scan before moving on to deal with the next arrival.

In these early days they had to make their way to Moria camp to register and be able to move on to the mainland. The first impression of Europe for so many thousands was high concrete barriers, barbed wire fences and chaos. Lines for food, lines for water, lines for toilets and lines for information. The conditions would not have been fit for animals, and anyone who stayed in Moria was forced into full survival mode. It was a place of shadows and danger, where children slept on the concrete floors, where parents struggled to keep their families together amidst the crowds.

There was an urgency to everything as the rumours reached us on Lesbos of borders further north in Europe threatening to close. Families wanted to move as rapidly as possible off the island and onward to their hoped-for destination as soon as they had their papers. They would have to hike through the wintry mountains of Macedonia and Serbia and Austria without stopping. It was our job to make sure they had warm clothes, socks and a tent before leaving on this arduous journey. We filled bags with scarves and sweaters, stuffed energy bars and first aid kits into pockets and waved off hundreds of ferry boats full of determined people.

Then, like a door that slams shut, the powers that be implemented the Europe–Turkey agreement. From that point on anyone who arrived on Greek soil would be subject to deportation back to Turkey. There would be no freedom of movement off the islands. No-one was allowed to move on into the rest of Europe. Camps began to fill up, no-one being able to leave. Deportations back to Turkey happened only sporadically and then stopped. There was no way forward and no way back.

Politics tend to focus on immediate "solutions" rather than the root of a problem. Regardless of borders closing and boats being intercepted, the reasons why men, women and children fled remained the same. Wars still raged, persecution and poverty never ceased and the camps on the island began slowly and relentlessly to fill up again.

My work changed. Instead of responding to emergencies and filling gaps where we saw them, we had now to shift our focus to camps that had become permanent holding facilities. In an emergency it is easy to forget that the crowd is made up of individuals, but here in the camps the individual became visible again – all of their hopes and dreams, all of their fears, all of the trauma and all of their stories with time stretching out in front of them without any prospect of change.

The media spotlight had moved on, most of the volunteers went home, and again it was up to the people left on the ground to respond to these fresh challenges. The camp of Kara Tepe (black hill in Turkish) was created to serve the needs of the most vulnerable cases, including single-parent families, the wounded and the sick and the survivors of shipwrecks. More than half of the residents were children under the age of twelve. Steadily and with huge effort, Kara Tepe began to feel like a village. Social spaces, community kitchens, football pitches and mobile classrooms popped up all over the terrain. There was music again and art and colour. Visiting theatre groups and clowns entertained the children, there were movie nights and dances and concerts.

Children became children again. In the early phases of the crisis, it was apparent that even the smallest children had had to grow up much too fast. They had years of war behind them, had witnessed untold horror and had seen the fear in the eyes of their parents. They had missed school either partially or altogether. Their bodies were underdeveloped, their teeth were usually blackened and often missing. They had nutritional as well as developmental deficiencies. They were given the care of younger siblings so that their parents could spend whole days standing in line for basic supplies and asylum information. They were serious little adults with tight faces and tough exteriors.

In Kara Tepe children could embark on the journey back to their childhoods. There was not much in the way of resources, but children are resourceful. Guy ropes become skipping ropes, cardboard boxes become clubhouses. They played house under containers and trucks. They lured kittens from behind

Amal prepares to land in Chios at dusk

the food trucks and gave them milk in bottle tops. They taped and retaped deflated footballs and played marbles for hours. They were hungry to learn and within months of working in Kara Tepe I was astounded to hear the children speaking Greek, English and even Dutch.

But, it was not a place where anyone wanted to stay. The insecurity of their futures and the weight of their pasts made visible the hidden torments that plagued everyone.

The older children and teenagers dealt differently with their pain. Teenagers often cut themselves at night. An incomprehensible release of deep, internal pain. It was common to see these lovely young people with bandaged arms and wrists. News would come from home, far away messages and videos on their mobile telephones would drive them to

despair. Among so much suffering and so much uncertainty, there was no space or rest truly to treat these wounded minds.

Down the road from Kara Tepe the walls of Moria still loomed. The camp filled up again, and because other safe spaces were at or over capacity, newcomers became stuck inside Moria. The situation deteriorated to the point that we anticipated that something catastrophic would happen. Smoke could frequently be seen rising between town and Moria camp. A faulty wire, a tipped-over stove, a garbage container in flames, another row of flimsy tents burned to ash. There were riots and demonstrations. There were heavy-handed police reactions. The stink of tear gas and of smoke, the smell of sewage and garbage were everywhere. The population grew, year after year, until it reached more than 20,000 in a camp meant

Opposite and above: Amal is greeted by crowds in Chios

for 3,000. Every alarm bell and warning sign was ignored.

What at first was a humanitarian crisis is now a political one. It seems that the suffering and the sadness may be the point. Populist rhetoric and a hard-line government combined with the restrictions brought on by the corona pandemic have made the situation in Greece even more tense. The camps were put into a lockdown that stretched out indefinitely while the local population and the tourists had fewer restrictions. The new government made good on their election promises and began threatening the closure of any solidarity space in the country that was not a state-sanctioned facility.

In September 2020 messages started appearing that another fire had broken out in Moria. This time, however, it was not normal. The entire camp, the hillsides around it and all the shacks and tents within it went up in flames. Many thousands of people ran out to the streets in panic. They were caged in by the police and held out in the open air for two weeks without adequate water or food or shelter. Moria was no more. There were daily demonstrations calling for evacuation and freedom. The situation could no longer hold.

In response, Greece and the European government have built even bigger camps. The walls are higher, the barbed wire is now rolled out in multiple layers. The communities inside Kara Tepe have been evicted and all open structures that housed refugees

Amal walks the eight kilometres from the refugee camp of Katsikas to Ioannina. Her way is illuminated by more than 1,500 light boxes made by local artists

have been closed. Everyone is now behind a fence in a closed camp. Within those fences are still children, who dream of school and cake and cartoons and games. The political theatre is pulling at the strings again, and the futures of those caught inside these camps are more precarious than ever. The root causes of why people put children into fragile boats only for them to end up in prison-like camps have not changed. War, hunger and persecution prevail. There are still boats full to capacity setting out from the Turkish coast trying to reach Europe. But, now, they are mostly intercepted in the middle of the sea and disabled. They are literally pushed back over the maritime borders in defiance of law and the rules of the sea itself.

It has grown dark. Even the very symbol of these children, in the form of Amal walking through Greece, was met with stones and shouts of anger. The resilience and unflappable hope I always so admired in this place is fading. The mood inside the camps is resigned. No amount of outrage and energy seems to make an impression on the powers that control the fates of so many.

The spotlight of the world has moved on, the private donations have dried up and there is a general fatigue about all things "refugee". Yet it is intolerable that children live behind razor wire simply for having been born with the wrong passport. We cannot accept that the rights and protections we hold so dearly for ourselves do not apply to those who come seeking shelter on our shores.

I have allowed hopelessness to enter my heart and just as quickly I try to banish it again. Among the shadows and in the darkness, one sees points of light even more brightly than before. I hold on to those lights, they illuminate the way forward. Light in the defiant, love and welcome for Amal despite the threats, light in the simple and hopeful acts of kindness and solidarity given daily without fanfare. When I saw the parade of joy and wonder that followed Amal through an Athens neighbourhood, I remembered my own joy and wonder again. There is so much hope to be found in our humanity, in the way we share with our neighbours, care for our children, in truly seeing each other despite our surface differences. That is the place where our nature shines brightest and that is the place where hope springs eternal.

A quiet moment for the puppeteer Girum Bekele in an underpass as he prepares to perform in front of a potentially hostile crowd in Larissa

Top left, bottom left: Little Amal is met by protestors in Larissa. Top right: Amal in the underpass in Larissa.
Bottom right: A family unit in stress on the ground

Fidaa Zidan, a puppeteer, robes up for her first performance with Amal

Amal walks through a refugee camp made up of shipping containers

Amal is greeted by a refugee in the camp

Inside a temporary shelter, a family watches Amal pass by
Overleaf: Amal in silhouette at sunset just before her passage to Italy

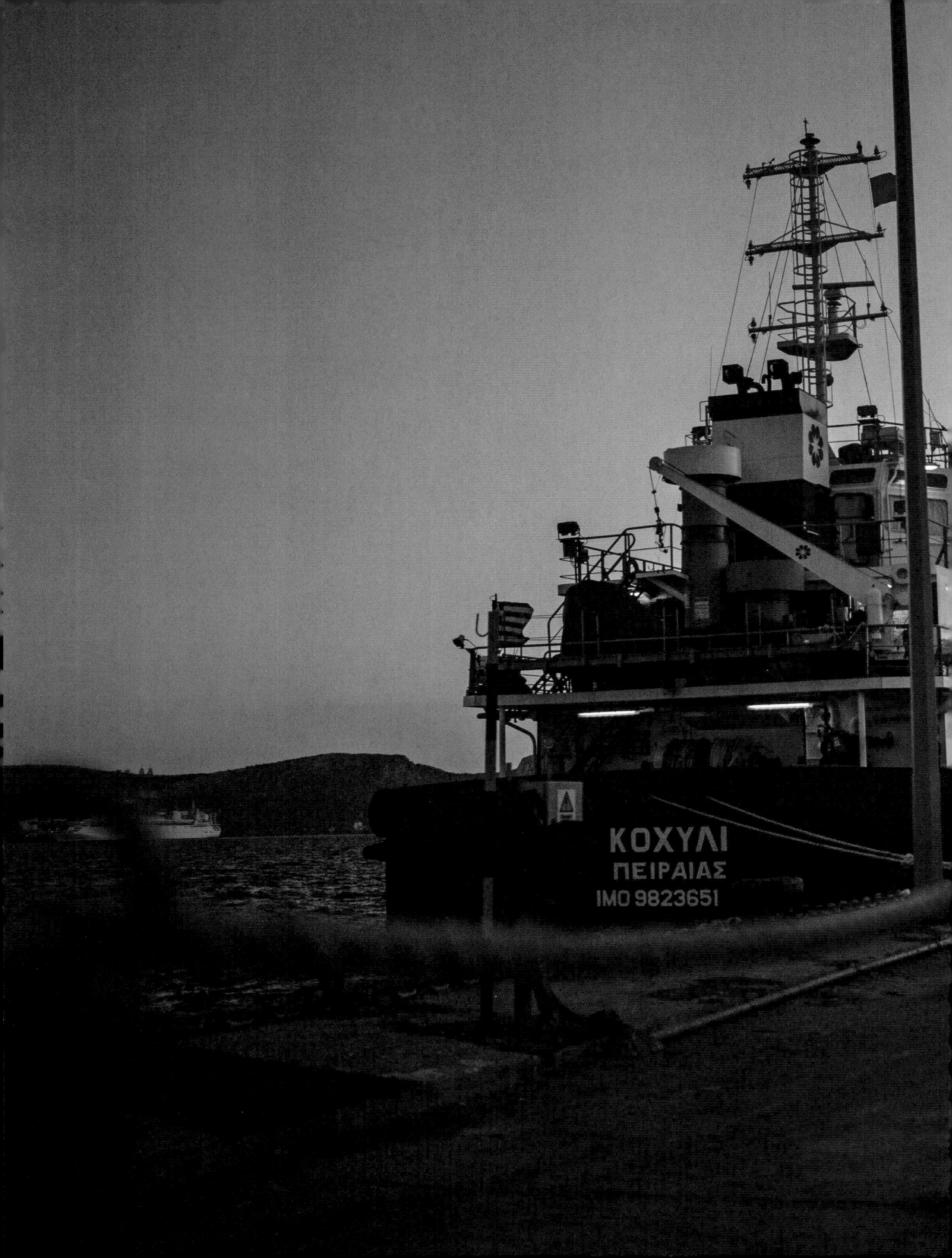
ΚΟΧΥΛΙ
ΠΕΙΡΑΙΑΣ
IMO 9823651

Italy

ERRI DE LUCA

A line in Virgil's *Aeneid* has remained with me from secondary school. It is spoken by Aeneas to Dido, Queen of Carthage, when she welcomes him after he is shipwrecked on her shores. Dido asks him how he has managed to save himself from the destruction of Troy, his home city. This crucial line comes in his reply: *Una salus victis nullam sperare salutem.* The only salvation for the defeated is not to hope for salvation.

This paradox is incomprehensible to anyone who has not had to tear themselves away from their homeland and look for some means of escape from the fray. They cannot understand what kind of salvation is possible without hope.

On the other hand, for anyone caught up in the flames, the meaning is hideously obvious. What use is there waiting for external help in the hope of rescue? The only remote salvation is to get the heck away from the hindrance of useless hope and to force a desperate way out of the flames.

I was reminded of Aeneas' words during the weeks spent on a rescue ship of the *Médecins sans Frontières* in the Mediterranean. Among the hundreds of people hoisted on board were women with babes in arms caught in the nick of time before their vessel sank.

What impulse is stronger than a mother's instinct to protect? What moved these women to risk the lives of their children? The answer is in the reply of Aeneas: to have no hope in the possibility of being saved. In its place explodes the energy of desperation.

Desperation is the motive force of today's migrations.

It is desperation that makes you climb at night into an inflatable rubber dinghy overloaded with mothers and babies. A mother's justification is the conflagration left behind. There is no barrier, no refusal of entry or mortal danger capable of stopping their journey.

The pilgrimage of this large marionette Amal from Syria to Europe is being undertaken in their image and likeness. It is not made of flesh, blood and desperation, therefore it can cross frontiers by day without having to travel at night, hounded by the police.

I hope it can be misunderstood in the way the Trojans mistook the wooden horse as a gift and discovered it held a force of Greeks. And that Amal and the force behind her may shock and upset until the collapse of the blinkered resistance that has turned the Mediterranean into the largest mass grave in its long history.

Translated from the Italian by N. S. Thompson

Opposite: Children crowd around Amal in Naples trying to hold her hand

Above and opposite: Amal explores Forcella, the historic district of Naples

Garlanded with flowers, Amal walks through Piazza della Sanità in Naples as she is celebrated by onlookers

A moment of reflection with Amal's shadow

Amal walks through the streets of Naples greeting people on their balconies

Opposite: Amal emerges from la metropolitana next to Vittorio Emanuele park in Rome, which is famous for being the city's centre of multiculturalism and tolerance
Above: Andrea Costa, head of the Baobab Experience Humanitarian Association in Rome

Above and opposite: Refugees in Rome. Without papers to work legally, these refugees have been forced to live on the streets. The Baobab Association provides language courses as well as tents, food and clothing

Amal embraces the "Angels Unaware" sculpture in St Peter's Square. It is dedicated to the world's migrants and refugees

Amal outside the Basilica of St Francis in Assisi

Pope Francis meets Little Amal in the Vatican City

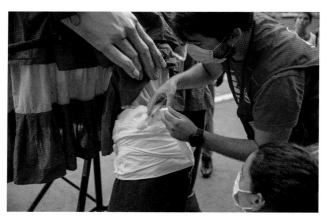

Amal plays with the girls and boys teams at Bologna F.C. She sustains a knee injury but still manages to save a goal

Rachel Leonard, a puppeteer, embraces Amal in Parco della Montagnola in Bologna

Amal is frightened by the fireworks that welcome her to Milan. Loud noises, fire and smoke have a different meaning for a child fleeing a war

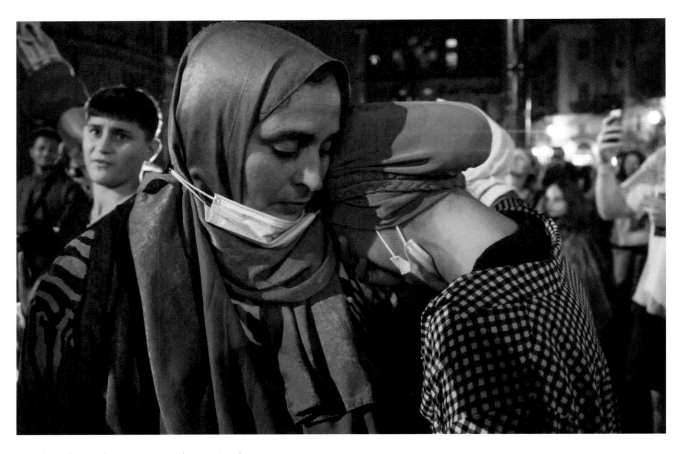

People gather in the streets to welcome Amal to Turin

France – South

Be us if not then what?

Amal Amal
Sister of paper cardboard paint and wood
Amal dear Amal our larger-than-life sister
Amal cherished doll welcomed in
Amal who moves ever onwards
Calm upright unshakeable eyes wide open to the world unfolding
Before you
Amal queen
Queen Amal
Whose name passes from mouth to mouth crossing borders cleaving
crowds prompting dancing cheers hope
Amal the name that from one person to another is murmured is
    spoken that offers a way through
Amal
And the countries the rivers the seas part before you
Benevolent beings watch you admire you praise you
Fête you
Caress you with their eyes their words their hearts
Amal sister of hope
Amal bearer of souls
Amal reliquary of dreams
Amal envoy of the voiceless
Amal
Will you tell them
Amal?
Tell them our names describe our faces our laughter our thousands
    of names faces

Opposite: Amal and a child at a beach event in Marseille

pupils fingers hearts

Lost to the watery depths

Will you tell them Amal?

You who stand there before them

A beautiful tree joyful and vivid magically concealing the rest of us

The forest of the dead

Amal will you cry out our death?

Amal will you shout out our death?

Amal will you beat

Your fists against the

Chests of all those joining you in your procession?

Will you claw at them bawl at them will you spew forth your bile?

Amal will you tell them the story of

The rest of us your fellow travellers your brothers and sisters accompanying
    you step by step

Invisible

Who are there alongside you

Who have become the stuff of your shadow

The fibres of the net in your tow

The wind in your wake

Will you tell them so they might look past you Amal

And see us in you through you

That they might hone their gaze to sharpen it

That they might carve open dissect slice apart the festivities the delight
    the carnivals

the processions

That they might split you in two Amal and reveal us

We the forgotten the nameless the dissolved the swallowed down

We who are rotting in your giant belly

We who are in

You who are pregnant with the rest of us

The dead

Men women and children

You who are weighed down by our lives cut short suspended struck from the

History of men?

If not to what end Amal?

To what end the circus the spectacle the parades the daily stages the
    welcoming committees the celebrations as you go on your way Amal?

To what end?

Tell them all you are not and everything we are

Tell them we are what you are not

More real than this reality

Open their minds Amal and lead us inside as if into a palace where we might make
ourselves at home

If only to soil it with our tattered garb tear-soaked and salt-encrusted from the sea
with our ragged bodies our decaying flesh worn away by the water gnawed at by
scavenging fish

Invite us in with all the heaviness of our awkward discomforting obscene
ugly cumbersome stinking cadavers

We were like you Amal

We were the same

We too were on an unreliable vessel

Overburdened with bodies

Children men young old women grandmothers labouring mothers newborns
mewling

People gathered together pressed tight huddled up and the waves around us
powerful and beautiful

Then simply powerful

Then ugly

Then all at once screaming horrifying tall so tall

And the sea took us between her jaws chewed us up

Dismembered us digested us and now we are no longer

We are no longer

We are

No longer anything

No name no body no past nothing else

Nothing Amal

But you

You exist

You can be us

Us through you

Us you

Us Amal

Yes be us

Amal

If not then what?

Translated from the French by Stephanie Smee

Overleaf: Amal is greeted by crowds at the Vieux Port Pavilion, Marseille

A dance is performed for Amal at Catalan Beach, Marseille, "When the Waves Have Come and Gone", remembering the loss at sea of refugees

Amal is offered cards of good luck by children in Marseille

Amal takes part in a parade, Marseille

Opposite, top left: Amal acknowledges a poster as an onlooker takes a photograph, Marseille
Opposite, top right, bottom and above: Amal with well-wishers in the mountains in Briançon

Above and below: Performers in Belfort

Amal looking towards Basilica Notre-Dame de la Garde, Marseille
Overleaf: Amal travels in her specially-made new box car, Marseille

Bethe: ...

Kusch: precise measurement ...

Powell: discovery of pi-meson ...

Gabor: theory of holograms ...

Goeppert-Mayer ...

ENIAC 1st electronic ...

$\mathcal{E} = mc^2$

Einstein

$\mathcal{E} = h\nu$

Planck

$6.626068 \times 10^{-34} \, m^2 \, kg/s$

Speed of Light

...mer and Huygens   220 000 000 m/s
(moons of Jupiter)

...9 Fizeau   315 000 000 m/s
(toothed wheel)

1862 Foucault   298 000 000 m/s
(rotating mirror)

1879 Michelson   299 796 000 m/s
(rotating mirror)

1983 17th CGPM   299 792 458 m/s (exa...
(definition of the meter)

$\mathcal{E} = h \cdot 10^{3} \, W$

Switzerland

TUESDAY REITANO

A dangerous journey: the securitisation
of migration and its deadly results

People across the globe are on the move at an unprecedented scale, driven by a whole range of forces: conflict, violence from criminal groups and social unrest, bad governance and persecution, climate change and its effects, unequal development and a dearth of ways to make a living, to live in dignity and in safety. Despite the lofty ambitions enshrined in the Sustainable Development Goals the reality is that for many the world already feels apocalyptical, plagued by drought, floods, desertification, suffocated by pollution, or punctuated by the sounds of gunfire and bombs and the constant fear of harm.[1]

The current global estimate from the International Organisation on Migration (I.O.M.) is that an estimated 281 million people, or 3.6% of the world's total population are migrants living outside their home country, and the scale of migration is accelerating: it is nearly double those on the move in 1990 and three times the estimated number in 1970.[2] Yet, even as the imperative and desire for mobility grows, the opportunity to do so safely and legally is increasingly being restricted, mostly to the educated and richer international migrant rather than those in the greatest of need. Refugees moving in large numbers from any one of the world's protracted and unresolved conflicts – Syria, Somalia, Yemen, Afghanistan, Iraq, Venezuela to name just a few – have found themselves unable to access the rights and privileges afforded to them under the 1951 Refugee Convention. They instead find themselves suspended in interminable, intergenerational holding patterns in squalid and underfunded camps in neighbouring countries, unable to return home, offered no alternative to resettle elsewhere. Those moving due to economic hardship or environmental pressures are offered not even this.

Even prior to the pandemic that now overshadows most other policy considerations, the options for legal movement had been closing down. The traditional

1. The Sustainable Development Goals were agreed in 2015 by the United Nations General Assembly. They are a collection of seventeen interlinked goals with the aim to address global issues including poverty, inequality and climate change. They are intended to be reached by 2030.

2. I.O.M., "World Migration Report 2020, Geneva", https://worldmigrationreport.iom.int/

Opposite: Amal with the sculpture "Wandering the Immeasurable", which pays homage to great discoveries in physics through the ages at C.E.R.N., Meyrin

choice destination states in Western Europe and North America had become overwhelmed by the numbers from the developing south seeking opportunities. Even the Gulf States, one of the dominant employers of migrant labour from Asia and Africa, had become more wary as the international community held them to account on labour standards and fair wages. In a number of countries, by no means for the first time in history, international migration had become not only politicised, but weaponised, used as a means to draw back from international obligations and longstanding consensus, to undermine democracy and inclusive civic engagement domestically, to persecute marginalised populations and as a justification for both state and non-state violence. A report published by the Ethical Journalism Network into global media depictions of refugees and migrants found that across the globe a weakening media economy and political bias drove the news agenda, too often granting disproportionate airtime to political views that came close to hate-speech, stereotyping and social exclusion of refugees and migrants.[3] Migration control – the capacity to prevent migrants continuing their journeys – has been used to leverage political concessions and generate foreign investment.

In this environment, and with duelling forces of increasing vulnerabilities and the restriction of movement caused by the pandemic exacerbating the pre-existing pressures, human smugglers have become the shadow travel agents of irregular migration. It is this underworld service provider who determines not only who moves, how they move, where they move to and the route they take, but also the safety and security of the migrant along their journey is largely in their hands. With the rights and protections to migrants being eroded or ignored,

and borders closed or reinforced at least in part due to COVID, smugglers are more in demand, more powerful and more deadly than ever before.

The I.O.M. estimates that at least 45,000 people have gone missing on their migration journeys since 2014. Nearly 23,000 have died in the Mediterranean, at the doorstep to Europe, 5,500 have died travelling between north and south America, 10,000 have died in Africa, mostly journeying across the Sahara, and 4,000 have died in Asia while fleeing conflict and persecution.[4] Others have endured incredible hardship: being trafficked for sexual exploitation or for labour, being raped, kidnapped for ransom, extorted and abused.

But the responsibility for the suffering of migrants falls equally at the door of states and their policies, as well as the illicit enterprises that move them. The twin compacts endorsed in 2018, the United Nations' Global Compact on Refugees and the Global Compact for Safe, Orderly and Regular Migration, renewed the commitment of states to uphold and protect the rights of those on the move, as well as to address the human smuggling phenomenon. By failing to provide adequate or sufficient means for people to move safely, legally and with dignity, so migrants are compelled into using illicit means.

Regrettably exacerbating the problem further, most states have opted for a criminal-justice-led, securitised approach to human smuggling, often backed by military power and in violation of human rights and other conventions to which those states have acceded. For example, warships were deployed in the Mediterranean to address the flows of asylum seekers from Libya and Turkey, and the United States has much more than $100 billion on countering illegal immigration, and deploying a paramilitary force in service of border control. One could also cite the Australian policies of off-shore detention and

3. Ethical Journalism Network (2015), "Moving Stories, International Review of How Media Cover Migration", http://ethicaljournalismnetwork.org/assets/docs/054/198/8feb836-108e6c6.pdf

4. I.O.M., "Missing Migrants Project", https://missingmigrants.iom.int, accessed November 2021

the practices of push-backs deployed by the littoral nations in the Andaman Sea as further examples of these policies of punitive deterrence against those on the move.

Such an approach drives the smuggling market towards its most exploitative manifestations – the more risky the journey becomes, the more barriers put in place, the more necessary a smuggler becomes and the more risk-tolerant, criminalised, corrupt and expensive the smuggler will need to be to perform his function and help those on the move continue their journey. It is here that the self-reinforcing negative spiral comes into play. As a militarised response to irregular migration and human smuggling is enacted, the smuggling industry shifts across the spectrum from a community resilience mechanism to a corrupt, violent industry controlled by organised crime groups. With the involvement of organised crime, and the increasingly negative results that this implies, the use of typical strategies to counter organised crime are triggered by default. Law enforcement action is intensified, more walls are built, border guards deployed, and detentions and prosecutions quickly follow. Barriers to migration are raised yet again, and the industry hardens still further into its criminalised form.[5]

A lot of difficult thinking needs to be done to break this vicious cycle that only inflicts cruelty on those who are most vulnerable. From all corners of the globe come calls to offer new solutions and new approaches to the movement of people, regardless of the cause of their movement. The definition of those "refugees" needing international protection is widening and blurring, as we deal with persons fleeing urban gang violence, bad governance, poverty, inequality and environmental depredation, and states are falling short of their obligations even under the narrowest of categories. Furthermore, it is not

Amal visits the United Nations, Geneva

sufficient to heap opprobrium on failing states – the structures of mobility are changing, and the framework of policy needs a radical rethink with an acceptance of mixed movements of migrants and refugees as the norm.

There is a rational pragmatism to people's drive to relocate and to seek to build a life in new places – they seek to replace a situation that has become untenable for one in which they have a chance of building productive lives for themselves and their families. They do not tend to stay in places that cannot support them, where they cannot find work or safety. Facilitating a system by which the states with the economy and population that can productively absorb migrants, with all the entrepreneurism, spark and culture that these pioneering populations have historically travelled with, is a far greater guarantee of global security, than continuing to build walls to prevent their movement.

5. Peter Tinti and Tuesday Reitano, *Migrant, Refugee, Smuggler, Saviour*, London: Hurst Publishers, 2016

Germany

TIMUR VERMES

Summer 2021. What an idea. Executed with the minimum of effort to raise awareness of the refugee issue once more. Organised by a mere handful of people. A simple journey across Europe. And, at the end, an initiative that causes a sensation, arouses sympathy, but also provokes anger, even outrage. The feat of those behind it must be acknowledged.

Or, more accurately, the feat of the man behind it. Alexander Lukashenko.

The Belarus autocrat simply picked a few dozen refugees from Afghanistan, Iran – he did not care where they came from. He had them taken to the borders of Poland, Latvia and Lithuania, and then nonchalantly watched E.U. states allow helpless people to suffer and die only a few metres from their borders. An astonishing coup, unscrupulous and clearly the action of an arsehole, but a political and media triumph nonetheless. And even more remarkable given the difficult time in which it took place.

Let us recall that prior to this, the refugee question had faded substantially in the public's consciousness and was no longer a hot topic. First it was something we simply got used to, then it was displaced by an issue of similar urgency. "Fridays for Future" is a movement born of another fundamental crisis. It is new, brimming with ideas, easier on the eye, better organised, finds fluent expression in a multitude of languages and is neatly captured on camera. And whereas the (justified) desire of refugees for a better life always has – and must have – elements of selfishness, the children protesting against climate change unquestionably want a better world for everyone. Then the refugees found themselves overtaken by COVID too, a worldwide pandemic, unstoppable and life-threatening. There were empty streets, lorries full of bodies, the vision of New York in lockdown, images never before seen. What did refugees have to rival that? Nothing save their own helplessness, the same old boats, the same old camps, the same old corpses and the same old unpleasant realisation that we who view these pictures are incontrovertibly complicit, because of our lethargy and our prosperity that is so damned appealing. A bitter, uncomfortable, painful truth that nobody likes to hear, which is precisely why the effectiveness of Mr Lukashenko's P.R. campaign was so striking. He chose the right narrative at the right time.

He didn't rely on arguments.

Opposite: Amal walks among the crowds outside Cologne Cathedral

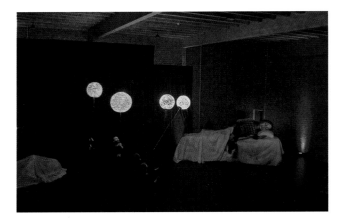 

Above, opposite and overleaf: Amal with the DUNDU (translated as "you and you") family of illuminated puppets in Stuttgart

But on our fears and egoism.

Lukashenko's stunt exposes what has been happening in Europe since the summer of 2015: nothing, less than nothing. Europe has dithered and put the brakes on whenever possible. Yes, Europe has spent money, but not to solve their own problem or that of the refugees. Rather the money has gone on putting obstacles in their way. Including the most idiotic of obstacles, we might add, for if you make yourself dependent on a political gambler like Erdoğan it's obvious that he will manipulate as much and as often as he likes. Then it's only a matter of time before every small, medium and large criminal all the way to Alexander Lukashenko has understood that they too can use refugees as bargaining chips because it's a great way to blackmail the E.U.

There might have been the flimsiest legitimacy for this junk policy of blocking, had Europe used the breathing space to work out a reasonable and sustainable solution compatible with the principles of Western democracy. Lukashenko's stunt, at the bargain price of a few thousand litres of petrol, demonstrated that nothing of the sort happened, not even in Germany, which should have been the first country to devise a solution. Because being the richest state, Germany is the most susceptible to blackmail.

This is all the more surprising given Germany's recent success story. You take in migrants, train them in the spirit of Western democracy with all its entrepreneurial freedoms, and some of them go on to develop a COVID vaccine. BioNTech, the company established by two children of migrants, made a turnover of two billion euros, and that was in the first quarter of 2021 alone. A one billion euro profit. Two thousand jobs. Which equates to tens, hundreds of millions of euros tax from the company and its employees. Education and training, and Western values – this is the fertile ground for those societies to which most people flee if they have to.

And that, in a nutshell, is the solution, perhaps the only solution with a genuine chance of being implemented. Because it doesn't appeal to kindness, magnanimity or goodwill, but to the only trait that can reliably overcome fear and hesitancy: greed. It needs to be hammered home to people that refugees and human rights aren't a huge financial burden that will gnaw away at their ever-dwindling fortune. On the contrary, they are the only way to ensure this prosperity will still exist tomorrow. We must be made to see the potential riches in the big and small BioNTechs, and not just in the firms themselves, but also in the people whose contribution to our society is limited by what they are permitted to do. We have

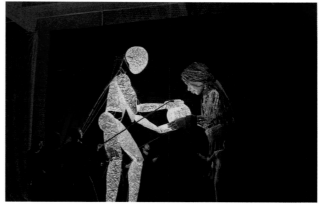

to understand that migration can be extremely lucrative if you manage it as a highly professional destination country rather than as a people trafficker. If you train tens of thousands, hundreds of thousands of people just as a football club would its up-and-coming talents. Although you never know who will turn out to be really good, you nurture all of them, because that is how you produce prohibitively expensive international players, top league players, players in lower leagues – as well as an enormous number of others who at least know the rules of the game. And meanwhile you're replenishing club funds – in our case, the ramshackle pension system. This is the refugee story that needs to be told, that needs to be worked out before the electorate screams at its politicians: "How long are you boneheads going to leave this money lying around in the streets."

It would be the story that would have the Lukashen-kos, Erdoğans and Orbans of this world chasing their tails, while also ensuring that we always have sufficient lorry drivers – for petrol, turkeys and other little things. The story that means it is only a matter of time before other countries wonder why they are not doing the same. Or why all this time we have asked for compassion, when it would have been far easier to say, "We're going to offer you a massive deal. And the first of you to seize it will have the greatest head-start."

Amal hasn't told the story of big money either. You cannot expect that of a big little girl. I've enjoyed watching her. There have been lovely moments, and poignant ones, my favourites being the minor encounters – not when Amal has been walking in a throng of dancers, but meeting individual people, spontaneously, unrehearsed, confusing and entertaining. For all her friendliness and cuteness, however, Amal has put one thing in sharp focus: the extent to which we have pushed the migration issue into the background.

In 2015, on the beach in Bodrum, the photograph of a young boy elicited sympathy around the world.

To elicit the same sympathy today you need a refugee child three and a half metres tall.

Translated from the German by Jamie Bulloch

Above and opposite: Amal meets people in the streets of Cologne
Overleaf: Amal joins dancers outside the cathedral in Cologne

Above and opposite: Amal is given a present of a suitcase and joins the community musicians in a celebration in Ehrenfeld, Cologne

Opposite, above and overleaf: Ruhrfestspiele Festival and the local community in Recklinghausen greet Amal with paper birds, painted pebbles and messages of welcome. The painted stones will be part of a huge constellation to create a permanent sign of safe passage for refugees

Belgium / The Netherlands

MARIEKE LUCAS RIJNEVELD

There goes the refugee child, the emigrant,
the girl who has no home, making her way
along roads that may be impassable, her feet
ruined for fortune, for palmy days, safety

and a warm maternal lap. She searches
as stars appear in the sky, as darkness
slips into his wolf suit and howls in her ear.
All the miles she has walked, all the people

she has spoken to, but nowhere among them
her mother's gentle voice, nor her everything-
will-be-alright promise that has turned into a
marching song inside her head. Sometimes

she's afraid she's running in the wrong direction,
that her compass points her to an even more
violent land, or that the sea she's heard about
doesn't exist, that she'll never reach England,

Opposite: Amal celebrating with a dancer her arrival in Antwerp

and instead be engulfed by dark clouds. Yet there
is hope, since however much they've belittled her,
however many fists have been shaken at her back,
she has grown, her shoulders are those of a giant

now. If you spot her in the distance all you have
to do is call out her name: Amal! Amal! Open
the borders, open your arms – one day she will
find a home where her dreams are undisturbed.

Translated from the Dutch by Michele Hutchison

Above: Amal attracts onlookers in Brussels
Opposite: Dancers, parkour and circus artists at Anderlecht Abattoirs, Brussels create a performance exploring
Amal's traumatic memories of home
Overleaf: In Brussels, Amal is chased through the streets by her memories. Wherever she looks, the ordinary
becomes threatening

School children welcome Amal to Brussels

Amal entering the Church of St John the Baptist at the Béguinage, Brussels. L'Union des Sans-Papiers pour la Régularisation campaigns for the recognition of the rights of undocumented people

Women with banner, "We are also human", in the Church of St John the Baptist at the Béguinage, Brussels

Above, opposite and overleaf: In Antwerp, Amal is welcomed by Hetpaleis Theatre Company. Their encounter explores the experience of newly arrived refugees in the city

Above, opposite and overleaf: Amal in Antwerp

Amal crosses the French border in an event organised by the people of Bouillon

France – North

OLIVIER NOREK

Author's note: Nothing in this story is invented. It comes from several testimonies I heard when I spent some weeks in the Calais "Jungle", just before it was pulled down.

THE CROSSING

Midnight, somewhere near Calais, France

The cafeteria in the last service station before the Calais ferry Customs. Pallid neon operating theatre lights, garishly-coloured magazines, stuffed toys for parents guilty of forgetting teddies, rows of chilled triangular sandwiches. On edge, the driver burned his throat on a last mouthful of bad coffee.

He glanced out at his lorry a few metres away, one of its rear doors deliberately left open. He'd been paid a great deal to do that. Shadows emerged from a ditch – one, then two, then ten. Among them Ayman, a boy from a village in Sudan some five thousand kilometres away. Five thousand kilometres, and he had risked his life at every one of them. Now he only had fifty left finally to reach the U.K., where he had been told that people were so kind they opened their front door to you and welcomed you into the bosom of their family. This wasn't the first time Ayman had been lied to, and yet if some day he discovered it, this one would be his greatest, most painful let-down. But we're not there yet. Not by a long way.

Don't ask Ayman how he got together the thousand euros the Afghan people-smuggler had demanded for him to climb into this lorry; it would break your heart. Just be aware that in the Jungle's brothel – because there is one – the price is five euros an adult, and ten if a child is more to your taste.

Don't ask him either what, between his village and France, he has been forced to do, to suffer, how often he has clenched his fists, or his blood rather than his tears has flowed. How often he has wondered whether it wouldn't be better for him to stay sitting there, in a filthy corner of the planet, waiting to die. Your soul would melt if he told you.

Under cover of a moonless night, the group of migrants reached the lorry, opened the rear door wider, and crept inside.

"Get in! Down to the front!" whispered one of the Syrians also trying his luck, pushing Ayman forward.

The kid did as he was told, clambering between stacks of boxes, partly feeling his way, partly lit by the telephone torch of the man in front of him. He settled between two pallets. Crouching there, he waited for all the others to climb on board and watched the

Opposite and overleaf: In Charleville-Mézières Amal encounters a group of young people who, like her, are carrying large suitcases door closing like a coffin lid. They were plunged into complete darkness.

The sound of breathing, the smell of fear, pushing and shoving to make some room, to hide as best as possible. Then the lorry started up. Nothing to do but wait. From the service station to the ferries, from the ferries to the dreamed-of England.

A few minutes later, and the driver embarked on the last stretch of his journey to the Customs. He slipped between two other gigantic vehicles in the fast track, and put his foot down. At the end of the main road leading to the gates of Calais, he drew near the first checkpoint, which looked just like an autoroute toll. Six lanes, six booths, and fifty or so lorries in a tarmacked area of two square kilometres, crisscrossing so often it made you giddy. Access lanes, exit lanes, private international lanes, French and U.K. Customs, contractors, border police. Even for someone accustomed to it, the place gave the confusing impression of a labyrinth, made worse by the dark night. The driver pulled into the third lane, and forced himself to be patient. Behind him, all Ayman could hear were anonymous shouts – he had no idea what they were saying. Every three minutes, the lorry advanced a few metres, parallel with several others.

Stern voices rang out so close to him he jumped.

"Shall I use the CO2 detector?" asked one of them.

For these men, women and children, the simple fact of existing, of simply trying to survive, to leave their hell, seems to upset many in Europe. That night, the simple fact of breathing CO2 in and out of their lungs could mean the end of their journey.

"They're covered with tarps, so air can circulate, which means they won't work. Go straight to the 'truffles'."

A few seconds later, the boy heard the panting of dogs straining at their leashes. Their paws dug into the asphalt, then pressed against the tyres to gain height and sniff the loads. The tyres? Their tyres?

A bark. Then another. Ayman clung to his tiny backpack like a lifebuoy.

"Positive over here!"

The boy was expecting the rear doors of his lorry to swing open and for probing torches to sweep the interior. And yet he remained in complete darkness. Anxiously, he lifted a flap of the tarpaulin and saw, less than a metre away, bathed in the yellow light from the booths, a couple climbing down from the next lorry. After spending more than a year in the Jungle, Ayman recognised them. Somalis. Good people who had once given him food.

"Out! Out! Out!" barked one of the officials.

A man and a woman, arms raised like bank robbers caught by the police, with their whole lives on the ground in two enormous sacks.

"Get out of here! Go away!" the Customs officials went on barking.

Ayman felt a blow on his back, and one of the other migrants lowered the tarp. He breathed again when he felt a slight jerk: their lorry was moving on to the second control point, thirty metres away. Too many migrants, not enough sniffer dogs. One lottery among many. Fresh voices could be heard.

"Checklist of your load, please. What are you carrying?"

"Computer spares and photocopiers," said the driver.

The Customs official ran his finger down the manifest then looked round wearily at the fifty other trucks arriving, themselves only the first wave of fifty more. But he was joined by a colleague, bringing a new toy that was finally going to relieve the boredom. He took a decision that seemed to amuse him.

"Pull over, monsieur."

Doing as he was told, the driver turned the wheel, cursing the fact that he had been willing to risk his job for a few thousand euros. He would swear he hadn't seen anything, that he couldn't check what was on his lorry after every traffic light, every café, every

Amal is welcomed at the "Porte de Calais" at Fort Nieulay

regulation break. He'd tell them he was the first victim of these foreign parasites who changed his driver's job into one controlling mass migration.

"We've got the same toy as the English," the Customs man explained to his colleague. "It's our chance to test it!"

After the lorry parked up, six small magnetic metal pads were placed on various parts of the bodywork. Each of them connected by cable to a computer terminal the size of a supermarket trolley two metres away. The Customs official adjusted the frequency of the detectors so that they picked up only one sound. Heartbeats. The English called this new piece of kit the "heart beat detector" and it was incredibly effective. You no longer had to open a lorry, search, pull out the boxes and pallets: this new technology had made their lives much simpler. To think that,

somewhere in the world, people had been up all night imagining and constructing this machine, then presenting their project, no doubt with a touch of pride, to other people, who had applauded and got out their cheque books.

Ayman's heart was beating so hard in his chest it almost hurt, but it wasn't audible. On the computer screen, however, it was an earthquake appearing at regular intervals. The earthquake produced by the heart of a petrified child and his companions.

"I've found a pulse!" the Customs man announced, like someone discovering a hidden treasure, a star, or solving a mystery.

"I've found a pulse!" The phrase normally uttered when someone is trying to save a life, now implied a much less happy outcome.

The rear doors of the lorry were opened and the

Customs officials waited for their quarry to emerge. One man, another, another, still more, heads bowed, arms full of their meagre possessions. A kick up the backside, a violent push...

"Get out of here! Get away, or we'll arrest you!"

An empty threat, because no court, police station, or prison would want them. Migrants – not people, simply headaches. Round them up, and send them where? Even their own countries don't want them.

"There's one left!"

A Customs man climbed inside, made his way to the front of the lorry, found a leg and pulled on it, cursing this last clandestine passenger who wouldn't come quietly. He squirted him with tear gas and waited for the poison to take effect.

Ayman gave in and crawled out of his hiding place. When they saw this terrified child, the officials looked at one another, more embarrassed than usual. Became human again.

Ayman came to the back of the vehicle and sat on the edge. His eyes red, his throat on fire, surrounded by giants. One of them shouted at him, gesticulating as if he was trying to drive away a dog and abandon it.

"Go on. Don't stay here. We're not going to adopt you. Go away, for fuck's sake!"

But Ayman just sat there, peering from face to face, uncertain whether they were scolding him, threatening him, ordering him not to move, or on the contrary telling him to clear off. One of the giants seized his arm to pull him down. It hit him like an electric shock: without thinking, the hunted child began to run, bewildered by the concrete labyrinth, past the first control booths, jumping at every dog barking, caught in the beams of torches. He saw a

Amal with police and crowds on the streets of Calais

gate in the distance and a line of lorries. To the drivers' astonishment he sped down it, zigzagging between the heavy trucks, slipping under a trailer. At last he found himself on the road out of Calais. Although his leg muscles were painful from sitting cramped in a corner for more than an hour, he ran until he was panting for breath, without turning round or slowing up for a single instant.

His blood was pounding in his temples, his breath coming in short, rasping gulps, as if the air was no longer breathable. He found it hard to see. He ran on almost blindly, and when the headlights of a thirty-three tonne monster dazzled him, the violent light became huge flames as everything around him caught fire. He heard shouts coming from his home village, their roofs burning in a black cloud of ash, and the rattle of submachine-guns. His lake swollen with the blood of his brothers and sisters: his lake,

the White Nile. He heard his mother's voice and her last words to him:

"Leave, Ayman, leave..."

Ayman, "the lucky one" in Arabic.

That was five thousand kilometres away. And he still had fifty to go to reach an England that didn't want him either. If some day he discovered that lie, it would be his greatest, his most painful let-down. But we're not there yet. Not by a long way.

He collapsed unconscious by the side of the road, on yellowing grass fed on exhaust fumes. He would try again another day, when he had again collected the thousand euros the people smugglers demand for each attempt. But above all, don't ask Ayman to tell you how he'll get them. It would break your heart.

Translated from the French by Nick Caistor

Left: Following a treasure hunt, Amal reaches Fort D'Aubervilliers, where she meets a frog puppet and receives a present
Right: In Charleville-Mézières a family holds a placard that says "Help Syrian children to live a safe and dignified life"

Amal is given a book in Bobigny

Amal is welcomed in Bobigny by the company Les Grandes Personnes for an evening with Allebrilles in a parade of masks, floats and large illuminated puppets

Amal meets circus artists from the Micro Compagnie and LXS REYENXS in Parc de la Villette, Paris

In Paris Amal is welcomed to the stage of the Comédie Française by a resident actor, Gaël Kamilindi, who has himself experienced exile. He reads her a story and a poem on travelling, offering her the Comédie Française auditorium all to herself

Above and opposite, top: Amal is welcomed at the Théâtre National de Chaillot, Paris by acrobats from Compagnie XY, Paris

Amal continues her journey on the Seine, approaching Notre-Dame
Overleaf: Amal discovers an installation of tents in front of the Institut du Monde Arabe, Paris. Echoing the refugee camps, sounds of moments and memories of people from different parts of the world can be heard from each tent. The installation aims to combine hope with an uncompromising reality; what emerges is the singularity of each person, the identity and memory of what has been abandoned

U.K.

CRESSIDA COWELL

In the Footprints of Little Amal

In May of 2013, the footprints of five human beings were found in the sediment of a beach in Norfolk.

They were uncovered by a great storm, and stayed there two weeks before they were washed away, just long enough for a passing team of fellow human beings who happened to be scientists (an extraordinary coincidence – but that's another story) to recognise and date them to between 850,000 and 950,000 years old.

For we have been walking awhile on this earth, we human beings.

Walking, migrating, telling our stories as we go.

There is something extraordinarily touching about these footprints.

Two of the pairs of footprints were made by adults, an older man, and a young woman, and they are walking steadily, soberly, side by side across the beach.

But three of the pairs of footprints were made by children, and these footprints are *crazy*.

They zig-zag, they run around in circles, they loop the loop, they double-back on each other.

It is because the footprints are playing.

Why is this so moving?

As soon as we see that, as soon as we hear that, we are reaching back across time into the footprints of that family. Their children are the same as our children. We are divided by nearly a million years, and yet we are the same.

These are the oldest human footprints to have ever been discovered outside of Africa. So the ancestors of this family will have walked a long way to get here, possibly a similar walk to that which Little Amal has just taken, from the east, over the great European continent, all the way across the land-bridge called "Doggerland" that still connected south-eastern Britain to the mainland of Europe. They must have been dressed warmly, for the landscape that the family were walking through 950,000 years ago was cold, and very different from our own, a land of bison, hippos, mammoths, preyed upon by sabre-tooth cats and lions.

We don't definitively know what species of human being this family were. They were possibly "homo antecessor."

But we do know that the children of those human

Opposite: Amal has crossed the Channel and arrived in Folkestone

Left: Jude Law greets Amal. Right: Amal is greeted by the mayor of Folkestone

beings will have been dancing around, chatting, asking their endless questions, inventing games and stories, because we can see their footprints.

"Are we nearly there yet?"

We see those crazy footprints and we know they are like us.

That is what Little Amal is inviting us to imagine, as she makes her Long Walk across continents, across borders. She asks us to imagine, how is she feeling? Where is she going? What has caused her to make this walk, and how should we receive her when eventually she gets to us?

The details of the story are what brings the story alive for us. In Bologna, Little Amal falls over and hurts her knee. In Athens, she gets lost. In Naples, she is overtired, and has a tantrum.

Little Amal is the little made large, a challenge to us all, asking us questions, as children do all the time. And when we see her being made welcome wherever she goes, she gives us a vision of what could and ought to be.

This is what stories give us.

To quote Atticus Finch from Harper Lee's *To Kill a Mockingbird*: "You never really understand a person, Scout, until you consider things from his point of view... until you climb into his skin and walk around in it."

Writing and reading and listening to a story gives us a chance to walk around in someone else's skin.

And when you are writing for children you are walking the walk of the crazy footprints. People often ask me, when will you stop this crazy walk, and start writing for adults? As if that is somehow a more worthy, a more serious thing to do.

But what a privilege it is to write for children, dancing in their shoes, looking out at the world through the cool clear eyes of a child, and what a great deal you have to learn as an adult from that experience.

You think you are teaching *them*, and they are really teaching *you*.

Walking the walk of the crazy footprints takes you down the path of the truly important things in life, for these are the only things that children are really interested in. Love, death, adventure, what makes a hero, our relationship with the environment.

And playing. Playing is a serious business.

Children are experts at the game of walking in others' footprints. They do it all the time when they pretend to be someone they are not.

A child has not yet learnt the explanations, the excuses, the long and complicated reasoning that allows them to turn away from their understanding of our common humanity, and our responsibilities to others and the environment around us.

It takes an adult to do that.

Who is leading the current global protests against climate change, is it an adult, or is it a child? Of course it is a child, because only a child would ignore the impossibility of the questions they are asking, and the impossible answers that those questions then demand.

That is why the name "Amal", which means "hope" in Arabic, is so important.

Amal with crowds and paper puppets of birds, in the historic city of Canterbury

Amal on the steps of St Paul's Cathedral, London, is welcomed by children and faith leaders. She delivers a letter from Tarsus, the birthplace of Saint Paul

Children are experts in hope, and their belief in the impossible just might make it happen.

Until the impossible happens, and we provide the impossible answers to the impossible questions, let us hope the landscape around us will not take decades rather than a million years to change.

In the meantime Little Amal and those like her will have to keep on walking, in greater numbers than ever.

So we need to know how to greet her.

The instinct of a child is to welcome Little Amal. To ask her where she's going and why she's walking in the first place. To invite her in. It would be a very rare child who would turn Little Amal away.

Let's ask her questions.

"Where are you going, Little Amal? Why are you going there? What happened to your parents?"

And let's let *her* ask questions of *us*, too.

"How will you welcome me when I get to you?"

For the reasons Amal will be walking are only going to get more pressing.

So let us walk a while in the footprints of Little Amal.

Let us all hear her say "Don't forget about us".

Our own footprints will not last long on the beaches we are walking on.

And we are all Little Amal.

We know it in our hearts, it is just that we forget.

Amal visits Westminster Cathedral, London during prayer service

A group of women and girls take pictures and greet Amal at Westminster Cathedral, London
Overleaf: Amal on the Millennium Bridge on her walk around London, with St Paul's Cathedral in the background

Outside the National Theatre, London, Amal meets War Horse, who was also created by Handspring Puppet Company
Opposite: Amal celebrates her 10th birthday in London with a party at the Roundhouse and cake at the V.&A.
Overleaf: Amal closes her eyes on the giant bed made up for her in the Paul Hamlyn Hall, Royal Opera House,
while soprano April Koyejo-Audiger sings her to sleep

Amal celebrates the 150th anniversary of the publication of *Through the Looking-Glass* by meeting Alice in Oxford

A band joins the celebrations in Oxford

Illuminated dancers and crowds celebrate with Amal in Sheffield, the U.K.'s first City of Sanctuary for asylum seekers and refugees

Women greeting Amal at the Khizra Mosque and Community Centre in Manchester

Amal meets the crowds in Birmingham

Women Seeking Asylum Together welcome Amal home, Castlefield Bowl, Manchester

Manchester United Foundation welcomed little Amal to Old Trafford
Overleaf: Amal at her journey's end

My little r...
of hope,
You are s...
away fror...
It's cold t...
— stay wa...

ورى

Afterword

DAVID LAN

We're exploring the high-walled cobbled streets that twist through this ancient neighbourhood and open out onto a grassy square. We're looking for a quiet dead-end corner of this lively commercial quarter where our stilt-walking puppeteer can perch on a high stool and have the upper body of our very large puppet hoisted up over his head.

Focus, breathe, get into the character of a nine-year-old Syrian refugee girl, then to a cry of "puppet moving" stride out into the busy street for the first of the many events that have been planned to welcome Little Amal as she travels to villages, towns and cities along her 8000-kilometre journey in search of her mother.

It's day one of a three month journey. We're in Gaziantep in south-east Turkey, the city closest to one of the very few humanitarian crossings into and out of Syria, the Bab al-Hawa, "Gate of the Winds".

A man in a grey suit perched on the steps of his shop beckons to me. He has a child on his knee. The man is perhaps forty, but the lines on his face are deep.

"You wanting to buy silver? Come, see, very high quality."

He's from Syria.

"From which part?"

"Aleppo." Just like Amal.

"All these," his gesture takes in the stone houses with flimsy looking shutters and ironwork balconies and the shops with their pyramids of spice and rows of mannequins in wedding dresses and tuxedos, "all these people from Syria, every one."

The band from a music school are tuning up in the square. Families are stretched out on the grass, leaning up on their elbows, drinking tea.

Now it's dark. Amal appears hesitantly out of a narrow street into the square. There's a triumphant blast of brass and strings, music from her homeland to make her feel at home. Lasers placed on the roof of the hotel across the street spatter the walls of the castle on the hill with cascading flashes of light. It's a huge production number rehearsed over zoom for months for this single performance. . .

We can't walk our giant puppet through the streets of any city without the say-so of the authorities. In Gaziantep we're invited into the mayor's cavernous office. The floor is gleaming white tiles, the veneers on the tables shimmer like pearls. Happily, Madame Mayor is vigorously supportive. Amal's message to the world on behalf of millions of refugees, young and old, is "Don't forget about us." This chimes with the mayor's own message: "Don't forget what Turkey has done for the more than three million Syrian refugees who have found a home in our country."

In the coastal town of Mersin, Amal makes her now far more confident way along the wood-slat boardwalk, the breeze catching her long hair and making it fly. She gazes out at the sea. It is her first sight of it.

In a village high in the Anatolian mountains townsmen, all in the same baggy grey trousers, watch their wives and daughters sing a lullaby to Amal and stroke her brow as she rests from the first part of her journey. She's very tired and she still has a long way to go.

At Çeşme on the western edge of Turkey hundreds of pairs of shoes are scattered on the beach evoking the many who have lost their lives attempting to cross to Greece. The mayor joins Amal at the water's edge, gazing out at the island of Chios, a brief stretch of choppy water away. . .

She crosses to Chios on a rickety, rusty boat. As she climbs down from the boat and strides along the path that bounds the harbour it feels as if the whole town has come out to greet her. A band plays, a women's choir swells, on a balcony high above children jiggle marionettes and sing, a chorus of young people from a nearby refugee camp beat out the rhythm on the boxes they sit on and sing – all of them playing and singing the same song, a traditional welcome to the new year but with words rewritten to welcome Amal.

The Walk is theatre.

Did Amal actually cross from Çeşme to Chios? Yes and no. She did but dismantled and in her box as freight. Because of the pandemic human beings weren't allowed to arrive on Chios by sea so we filmed her setting out in the rickety boat and then brought her back. Instead of a 40-minute crossing, puppeteers and crew had to make the journey by air – Izmir to Istanbul, Istanbul to Athens, Athens all the way back across the Aegean to Chios.

So was it a lie to call Amal's journey The Walk? Yes and no. We walked for miles, perhaps hundreds over the months – I've never walked so much in my life – but no-one walked 8000 kilometres.

Was it challenging to organise the passage of twenty-five puppeteers, production managers, company managers, artistic directors and producers across eight countries during a pandemic? Of course it was, but obviously nothing like as difficult as it would have been if we were real refugees, not remotely. We slept in hotels, we had passports in our back pockets, even those of us who had been refugees at an earlier stage of our lives. And we were making the journey because we chose to.

Why did we so choose? Because once we'd had the idea – and especially once we'd understood that it shouldn't be "us" walking in homage to the millions who've made the terrible journeys, that it shouldn't be a pilgrimage but it should be theatre, that it should be a puppet of a child refugee who would lead us (Amal leads, we follow) we had no option but to do it. Not to do it would have been to deny to ourselves the reality of the world.

The Walk is a piece of public art in the way that a poem is a work of public art that demands its right to life as soon as it starts to take shape in your head.

In northern Greece a town council voted by 14 to 5 that our planned visit, for which we had permission from a regional authority, should not be allowed to take place. High above the town in the region of Meteora are ancient monasteries set vertiginously into the highest clefts of the mountain peaks. Amal was seen as a Muslim and wasn't welcome to walk on hallowed ground.

The theme of The Walk is welcome. Hundreds of artists had been invited to imagine how they might welcome a child refugee, exhausted, hungry, in radical need of care. Political and religious leaders at every level had joined in proclaiming through dance and music and film and theatre that, as the thousands thronging Deptford High Street sang out when we eventually arrived in London:

"Say it loud and say it clear:
Refugees are welcome here."

In another northern Greek city protestors threw eggs and fruit and, possibly, stones at Amal as she led a procession through the town. But further down the street were a far greater number protesting against the Greek government's policies. Their banners read:

"Close the camps, open the borders."

Amal arrived in Italy at the port of Bari. In a thousand-year-old courtyard the town band whooped it up. A Brazilian-Yoruba dance troupe, a Palestinian singer, marimba players. . . The acts followed joyously one after another until late into the night. Amal danced along, eyes closed, head thrown back as though exultant.

For some months we'd been talking to the Refugee and Migrant Department of the Vatican. Pope Francis has long spoken powerfully in support of refugees and frequently asks of believers that they "walk together". Would he meet Amal? The thought strikes us as outrageous. She's real to us but she's just a puppet, after all.

When we arrive in St Peter's Square a hoarding has been put up in front of a colonnade.

"Welcome Amal!"

As children from the neighbourhood play with Amal, a Cardinal makes a speech.

"Among migrants, children like Amal constitute the most vulnerable group. As they face the life ahead of them they are invisible and voiceless. Amal invites us to open our eyes and hear their voices."

We're led round the back of the soaring marble buildings through many gates and many doors, up a steep slope into a cooler world of towering medieval brick.

The children are led in vigorous song. They kick a ball about. Amal joins in.

Suddenly the Pope is amongst us. The children mob him shouting out "Francisco! Francisco!" as though he were everybody's favourite uncle.

Amal approaches, shy but towering over him. Pope Francis reaches up and, smiling broadly, takes her hand.

Contributors

AMIR NIZAR ZUABI is the artistic director of The Walk. An award-winning playwright and director, he was the founding artistic director of ShiberHur Theatre Company, and an international Associate Director of the Young Vic Theatre and a member of the United Theatres Europe for artistic achievement. He lives in Jaffa.

DAVID LAN is one of the producers of The Walk along with Stephen Daldry, Tracey Seaward, Naomi Webb for Good Chance Theatre Company and Handspring Puppet Company. Born in South Africa, he lives in London and the Languedoc. He was writer-in-residence at the Royal Court 1994–6, artistic director of the Young Vic 2000–18, consulting artistic director at the Performing Arts Center in N.Y.C. 2014–6 and is currently theatre associate at B.A.M. in N.Y.C. His publications include *Guns and Rain: Guerrillas and Spirit Mediums in Zimbabwe*, a volume of collected plays and a memoir *As if by Chance: Journeys, Theatres, Lives*.

SAMAR YAZBEK is a Syrian exile and an award-winning author and journalist. Her memoir *The Crossing* described her clandestine return to Syria to report on conditions during the war. She is a P.E.N. International Writer of Courage and won the P.E.N/Pinter prize for her first book *A Women in the Crossfire: Diaries of a Syrian Revolution*. In 2012, she launched Women Now for Development, an N.G.O. based in France that aims at educating children and empowering Syrian women socially and economically.

BURHAN SÖNMEZ is the President of P.E.N. International and the author of five novels that have been translated into forty-two languages. He was born in Turkey and grew up speaking Turkish and Kurdish. He worked as a lawyer in Istanbul before going to Britain as a political exile. He translated "The Marriage of Heaven and Hell" by William Blake into Turkish. He lectured in Literature at the Middle East Technical University in Ankara. He has won the Vaclav Havel Library Award and the E.B.R.D. Literature Prize.

LAURA JANSEN is a platinum-selling musician and songwriter. In 2015 she began volunteering in her hometown of Amsterdam when refugees arrived at the central station. This led her to Lesbos where she spent the next three years working along the coasts and in the camps. Her first book *We Saw a Light* is about the experiences at the edges of Europe. She is an independent advocate and storyteller who now uses her platform to engage with policy makers and the general public.

ERRI DE LUCA is a poet and activist whose awards include the Prix Fémina Étranger, the Prix André Malraux and the European Book Prize. His books have been translated into more than thirty languages, and he has been named "the writer of the decade" by *Corriere della Sera*. An actor, screenwriter and producer, he has been a jury member at the Cannes Film Festival.

PHILIPPE CLAUDEL is an award-winning French writer and film director of "I've Loved You So Long". He is a professor of Literature at the University of Nancy where he previously worked as a teacher in prisons. His novel *Grey Souls* won the Prix Renaudot and he was the winner of the *Independent* Foreign Fiction Prize for his novel *Brodeck's Report*.

TUESDAY REITANO is Deputy Director of the Global Initiative against Transnational Organised Crime. She was formerly the director of C.T. MORSE, an independent policy and monitoring unit for the E.U.'s programmes in counter-terrorism. She is the co-author of *Migrant, Refugee, Smuggler, Saviour* on the role of smugglers in Europe's migration crisis, and the lead editor of *War on Crime: Militarised Responses to Organised Crime*.

TIMUR VERMES is the Hungarian-German author of the satire *The Hungry and the Fat* about a refugee walk under the spotlight of television attention, for which in preparation, he walked hundreds of miles alongside refugees. His satire *Look Who's Back* sold more than a million copies in Germany. The film adaptation was a box-office hit and is available on Netflix.

MARIEKE LUCAS RIJNEVELD is considered one of the outstanding new talents in Dutch literature. In 2015, they made their debut with the poetry collection *Calf's Caul*, which was awarded the C. Buddingh' Prize. Their second collection *Phantomare* won the Ida Gerhardt Poetry Prize. Rijneveld's first novel *The Discomfort of Evening* won the International Booker Prize. It has been published in thirty-nine countries.

OLIVIER NOREK is one of France's bestselling writers of *noir* fiction, for which he has won many awards. For seventeen years he worked as a police officer in Paris Saint Denis. His novel *Entre Deux Mondes* is set in Calais' refugee camp, The Jungle. All of his books have been optioned for film and television and he was a writer on the T.V. series "Spiral".

CRESSIDA COWELL is the Waterstones Children's Laureate. She is the author and illustrator of the *The Wizards of Once* series, which has been translated into thirty-seven languages, and the *How to Train Your Dragon* series, which has sold more than eleven million copies in thirty-eight languages and is a major DreamWorks Animation film franchise, a Netflix series and a show on C.B.B.C. She is also an ambassador for the National Literacy Trust, the Reading Agency, a Trustee of World Book Day and a founder and patron of the Children's Media Foundation.

Acknowledgements

Amir Nizar Zuabi **Artistic Director**
David Lan **Producer**
Tracey Seaward **Producer**
Stephen Daldry **Producer**
Naomi Webb **Producer for Good Chance Theatre**
Basil Jones and Adrian Kohler **for Handspring Puppet Company**
Craig Leo and Enrico Dau Yang Wey **Puppetry Directors**
Joe Robertson and Joe Murphy **Founding Artistic Directors of Good Chance**

Puppeteers
Bartolomeo Bartolini, Girum Bekele, Sebastian Charles, Rachel Leonard, Emma Longthorne, Mouaiad Roumieh, Ben Thompson, Fidaa Zidan
Sarah Calver **Associate Puppetry Director**

International Producers
Claire Béjanin, Amaya Jeyarajah Dent, Yeşim Gürer Oymak for Istanbul Foundation for Culture and Arts (İ.K.S.V.), Yolanda Markopoulou, Roberto Roberto and Ludovica Tinghi, Recep Tuna

Production
Mathilde Andrieux, Tugce Aydin, Enrico Ballarin, Siham Belabri, Louison Bergman, Aida Bourdis, Nikos Charalampidis, Jack Dakar, Esra Dogruyol, Lucy Donald, Jack Ellie, Constantina Georgiou, Matilda Glen, Carla Guardascione, Suzy Hawes, Raphael Hillarion, Lizzy Jankowski, Daphne Kalafati, Aristeidis Kreatsoulas, Umut Kurç, Menelaos Kyparissis, Elina Lazaridou, Fiorella Lecoutteux, Lara Mastrantonio, Nick Millar, Sam Moore, Carla Mori, Diyo Mulopo Bopengo, marie Nore, Ece Öncü, Laurie Paul, Glyn Peregrine, Polyplanity Productions, Emma Puddy, Clara de Queiroz, Clement Riandey, Juliette Rizzi, Anna Ruiz, Alma Sammel, Laura Spiliotakou for Top Notch Travellers, Vicky Strataki, Zeynep Santiroglu Sutherland, Alex Sutherland, Annie Symons, Isil Terzioglu and Muge Erarslan, Emma Thiéblemont-Barusseau, Adreas Tsagronis, Monia Triki, Christos Tzamargias, Oona Viguerie, Connie Weber, Sarah Wright, Mehmet Yorulmaz and Özgüç Özgümüs for Ozyo Turizm Ticaret Limited Şirketi

Good Chance
Joe Murphy, Joe Robertson, Elizabeth Carpenter, Jo Cox, Hannah Harding, Medea Manaz, Dina Mousawi, Amy Reade, Mali Siloko, Connie Treves, Emily Webb

Drivers
Zakaria Baggour, Thomas Bireaud, Brian Braithwaite, Fabrice Caccamo, Angus Clark, Ziggy Duly, William Hunter, Ben Kramer, Shaun Martindale, Alan Perry, Sophien Johan Riahi, Charles Storer, Bernie Sullivan, Susie Sullivan, Souhaila Aicha Zahira

Kevin Fitzmaurice **Executive Producer**
Sarah Loader **General Manager**
Joanne Dixon **International Events Manager**
Philip Cowell **Head of Creative Development**
Layla Madanat **Assistant to the Artistic Director**
Alice Evans **Education Producer**
Shaun Evelyn **Head of Marketing**

Kate Jones **Company Manager**
Muaz AlJubeh **Technical Director**
Patrick Glackin **Production Manager**
James Dee **Puppetry Technician**
Natasha Savidge **Events Stage Manager**
Tristan Shepherd and Daniel Fazio **Producers for LOFT**
Jean Dakar and Elijah Grant **Videographers**

Documentary Team
Tamara Kotevska, Samir Ljuma, Martin Ivanov, Orlando von Einsiedel, Harri Grace, Guillaime Lopez, Antonia Moro, Tugçe Aydin, Ellie Braine, Roberta Canton, Siamak Etemadi, Baransol Boyraz, German Gomez, Seref Dikmenn, Manolis Makridakis, Vincent Pastor, Alessandra Salvatori, Jules Valeur, Janine Arce, Afraa Hashem, Yvonne Mihaylovich, Ariel Pintor, Defne Auf, Laura Vargas Villaveces

Press Representatives
Erica Bolton, Lara Delaney and Lauren Bolton for Bolton & Quinn, Funda Küçükyilmaz for Flint Culture, Michalis Strangos and Dora Marouli for MSComm Group, Allegra Seganti and Flaminia Casucci, Nathalie Gasser

Partners
A.S.B.L. La Source, Act 4, Active Arts, Municipality of Adana, Aikaterini Laskaridis Foundation, The Albany, Allianz Kulturstiftung, Association Alwane, A.M.A.K.A., Art Asyl, Khaled Alwarea, Alexandra Aron, Amare, Assitej Italia, Athens Comics Library, Municipality of Athens, L'Auberge des Migrants, AZ Celtic Films, Tammam Azzam, Balconnection, Baobab Experience, Barnsley Museum, Ammar al-Beik, Birmingham City Council, Birmingham 2022 Commonwealth Games, Birmingham Hippodrome, Bloomberg Philanthropies, District Borgerhout, Boy Blue Entertainment, BOZAR, MJC de Briançon, Mairie de Bray-Dunes, Canterbury Cathedral, Centro delle Arti della Scena e dell'Audiovisivo, Municipality of Çeşme, Change the Word, Chios Music Festival, Choose Love, Citizens of the World Choir, Citizens Theatre, City Lab, City of London Choir, Clyde Docks Preservation

Initiative, Comédie Française, Community Arts Network, Compass Collective, Complicité, Connect4Climate, Conservatorio di Musica Luigi Cherubini, COP26, Coventry City of Culture 2021, Creative Folkestone, La Criée – Théâtre National de Marseille, Dakos Films, Fondation Mahmoud Darwish, Ali M. Demirel and Balkan Karışman, Democracy and Culture Foundation Ltd, Municipality of Denizli, Dewynters, Dover District Council, DUNDU, Ville de Dunkerque, Elefsina Cultural Capital of Europe 2023, Emergency, Emergency Exit Arts, Emmaüs La Roya, English Heritage, Fablevision, Al Farah Orchestra, Festival Mondial des Théâtres de Marionettes, Firstep Productions, Folkestone Fringe, Fondazione Campania dei Festival, Fondazione Migrantes, Fray Studio, Future Foundry, Chiaro & Tondo di Domenico Galluzzi, Municipality of Gaziantep, Comune di Genazzano, G.L.A., Good Chance Theatre France, Grand Théâtre de Genève, Les Grandes Personnes, Greenside Primary School, Habibi Works, Samar Haddad King, Happy, Hellenic Children's Museum, The Hellenic Theatre/Drama Education Network (TENet-Gr), Hetpaleis, Humanity Crew, Impossible Productions, Festival Incanti, Institut du Monde Arabe, International Rescue Committee, International School of London, Municipality of Ioannina, İzmir International Puppet Days, İzmir Metropolitan Municipality, K2 Contemporary Art Center, Nadine Kaadan, Karam Foundation, Kent Refugee Action Network, University of Kent, Kingsway Park High School, Kırkayak Kültür, Alex Koch, Kültürhane, La MaMa Umbria International, Landsec, Lewisham Council, Lewisham Borough of Culture, Lewisham Refugee and Migrant Network, Liberté, Lieux Publics – La Cité des Arts de la Rue, LUSTR, Manchester International Festival, Manchester Street Poem, Manchester United Football Club and Foundation, Ville de Marseille, MAXXI, MC93, Municipality of Mersin, Mestiere Cinema, Migrants refugees, Migration Museum, Ministère de la Culture, Batool Mohammed A.K.A. OM.EL BEAT, La Monnaie, Mucem – Musée des Civilisations de l'Europe et de la Méditerranée, Mulberry School, Muqata'a, Muratpaşa Municipality Adalya Foundation Engelsiz Café, Musalı Village, Muse Creative, Museo e Real Bosco di Capodimonte, National Theatre, National Theatre of Scotland, National Trust, National Youth Dance Company, Nefes for Art and Culture, Network for Children's Rights, New York Times, One Young World, Orange Blossom Carnival, Parc de la Villette, Ville de Paris, Piccolo Nuovo Teatro – Teatro d'europa, Nuovo Teatro Sanità, Pears Foundation, Perth Theatre, Phosphorous Theatre Company, Piccolo Teatro di Milano, Municipal Theatre of Pireaus, Play for Progress, Project Everyone, Quaternaire, Rast Minus Design Initiative, Refugee Café, Refugee Tales, Remote Theatre Project, Mishcon de Reya, Rochdale Borough Council, The Roddick Foundation, Finn Ross, Roundhouse, The Royal Ballet, Royal Opera House, Ruhrfestspiele Recklinghausen, Omar Abu Saada, Sadler's Wells, St Paul's Cathedral, Maryam Samaan, Sanitansamble, Comune di Scampitella, Scène nationale, Municipality of Selçuk, SGDD ASAM, Shakespeare's Globe, Sheffield Canal & Riverside Trust, Sheffield Theatres, Mike Shnsho, Short Film Directors Association of Antalya, Sine Digital, El Sistema Greece, Somerset House, Sommerblut Kulturfestival, S.O.S. Méditerranée, Source ASBL, Southbank Centre, Still Moving, The Story Museum, Tamburo Rosso, Tarsus City Council, Teatro d'Europa, Teatro di Roma, Teatro di San Carlo, Teatro nel Baule, Teatro Pubblico Pugliese, Teatro Trianon Viviani, Théâtre de la Licorne, Théâtre des Marionnettes de Genève, Théâtre National de Chaillot, Théâtre National Wallonie-Bruxelles, Thessalian Theatre, TrasFORMAzioneAnimata, Municipality of Trikala, Underbelly, Unima Hellas, Unima Italia, U.V. Labs, V.&A. Museum, Vision Mechanics, Westminster Cathedral, Wigan Borough Council, Yaa Samar! Dance Theatre, Yaren Cooperative, Yellow Submarine Art Initiative, 350.org

Ambassadors

Waad Al-Kateab, Gillian Anderson, Kinan Azmeh, Joyce DiDonato, Noma Dumezweni, Chiwetel Ejiofor, Halit Ergenç, Jude Law, Gary Lineker, Ncuti Gatwa, Anish Kapoor, Youssef Kerkour, Bergüzar Korel, Magid Magid, Michael Morpurgo, Franco Nero, Yotam Ottolenghi, Onjali Q. Raúf, Elena Sofia Ricci, Katja Riemann, Philippe Sands, Anoushka Shankar, Juliet Stevenson, V (formerly Eve Ensler), Wolf Alice

Supporters

Amberstone Trust, Arts Council England, Asfari Foundation, Backstage Trust, Humphrey Battcock, David Binder, Maria Björnson Memorial Fund, Blavatnik Family Foundation, Comic Relief, Jeffrey Culpepper, A. Duffield, Elliot Foundation, Rasha and Hassan Elmasry, Emily's Garden Foundation, European Cultural Foundation, Esmée Fairbairn Foundation, Foyle Foundation, Sonia Friedman, Garfield Weston Foundation, Genesis Foundation, Antony Gormley, Greater London Authority, Calouste Gulbenkian Foundation, Agnes Gund, Roger De Haan Charitable Trust, Wendy van den Heuvel, I.H.S. Markit, Elizabeth Jack, Adam Kenwright, Omar Koc, Adel Korkor, Allianz Kulturstiftung, Fonds de Dotation Francis Kurkdjian, Kate Lear, Alexander Leff, Jonathan Levy, Linbury Trust, Patrick McKenna, Ministère de la Culture, Georgia Oetker, Ebru Ozdemir, Pack Foundation, PricewaterhouseCoopers, Remote Theater Project, Roddick Foundation, Ruddock Arts Foundation, Christine and Stephen Schwarzman, Lady Susie Sainsbury, Shapiro Foundation, S.H.M. Foundation, La Fondation S.N.C.F., S.N.H. Productions, Beth Swofford, The Talent Fund, Trudie Styler, Tides Foundation, Anda and Bill Winters, Susan Witherow, Barbara Whitman, World Bank Group

Special Thanks

Marielise Aad, Jad Abbas, Nicki Adams, Ammar Al-Beik, Ghufran Al-Taisnah, Nour Alwadin, Jumana Al-Yasiri, Michael "Mikey J" Asante, Johnny Autin, Marco Baliani, Mark Ball, Barut Kemer Hotels, Karen Bastick-Styles, Raphaël Benoliel, John Benton, David Binder, Georgia Bird, Sheriff Bob, Rosie Boycott, Rabbi Shoshana Boyd Gelfand, Diala Brisly, Annika Bromberg, Karen Brooks Hopkins, Tim Browning, George Butler, Sidi Larbi Cherkaoui, Cignpost Diagnostics, Sarah Cuminetti, Richard Curtis, Cardinal Michael Czerny, Marcus Davey, Giulia Delli Santi, Dorian Demarcq, Eric Deniaud, Diane Dever, Dial-a-Flight, Sherry Dobbin, Lord Alf Dubbs, Dynamic Shipping, Sean Egan, Eurofins, Nigel Evans, M.P., Sarah Ford, Giles Fraser, Maria Friedman, Alex Gladstone, Laura Griffiths, Sabrina Guinness and Sir Tom Stoppard, Nedjma Hadj Benchelabi, Ruth Hardie, Hope and Aid Direct, Damian Howard, S.J., Adrian Joffe, Jennifer Jones, Jean Kalman, Roxy Kamperou, Ezgi Ceren Kayirici, Jack Lang, Lanterns Studio Theatre, Phyllida Lloyd, Clare Lovett, Aymen Mahammednor, Claire Marshall, Justin Martin, John McGrath, Ruth McKenzie, Andrea and Beba Mingardi, Shaykh Ibrahim Mogra, Emily Morus-Jones, Anna Moutrey, Emma Noble, Rufus Norris, Lisa Oulton, Rachid Ouramdane, Cheryl Pierce, Fiona Pride, Jack Prideaux, Vanessa Redgrave, Miguel Rincon Rodriguez, Mark Rubinstein, Lord Russell of Liverpool, Mark Rylance, Karenjit Sahota, Kenrick Sandy, Mohamed Sarrar, Eric Schnall, R.P.M., Anil Sebastian, Lina Sergie Attar, Nick Skilbeck, Emma Stevenson, Simon Stone, John Studzinski, Justine Symons, Genevieve Tawiah, Sita Thomas, Connie Treves, Tysers, Anthony Van Laast, Oona Viguerie, Flaminia Vola, Emily Webb, Katrina Wesseling, Katherine Wilde, Felicity Willems, Rowan Williams, Revd Lucy Winkett, Rabbi Jonathan Wittenberg, Sarah Worsley, Lyndie Wright, Noor Zuabi